Your Wedding

PERFECTLY PLANNED AND PERSONALIZED

Your Wedding

Perfectly Planned and Personalized

Anthony DeMasi

Friedman Group

A FRIEDMAN GROUP BOOK

ISBN 0 7924 5742 0

YOUR WEDDING
Perfectly Planned and Personalized
was prepared and produced by
Michael Friedman Publishing Group, Inc.
15 West 26th Street
New York, New York 10010

Art Direction: Devorah Levinrad
Designer: Stephanie Bart-Horvath
Photography Editor: Christopher C. Bain

Typeset by Classic Type, Inc.
Colour separation by Bright Arts Pte. Ltd.
Printed and bound in Hong Kong by Leefung-Asco Printers Ltd.

To my one and only bride, Maria, and the best proof
of our marriage, Dianna and Jimmy

Contents

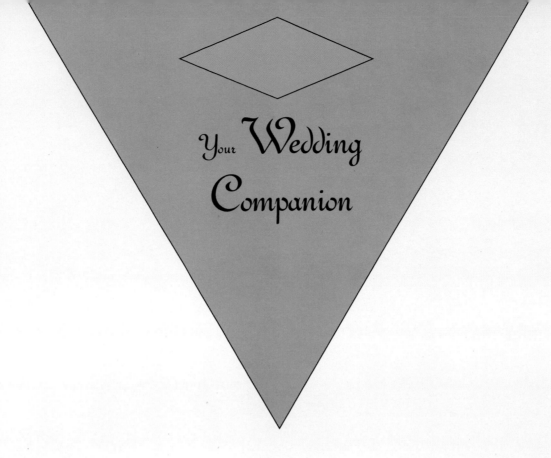

Your Wedding Companion

What day is it? The date really doesn't make any difference because the answer is always, "Someone's wedding day!"

Whatever the day, date, year, or even time; weddings take place. They don't happen by accident, though. Even the most modest or spur-of-the-moment wedding takes some planning; others will be so detailed you would think the event is to include a coronation! That idea isn't necessarily as strange as it sounds, because as tradition says, every woman is a queen and every man a king on their wedding day.

When do wedding plans begin? For some young ladies, the answer could be many years ago, when they saw their first wedding and in their hearts and minds started making notes of what would be part of their perfect day. More realistically speaking, wedding plans start with a question and an answer, namely: "Will you marry me?" and "Yes." Those simple statements start a race against the clock, and the finishing line is the ride to the honeymoon. Along the way, there will be many twists, turns, obstacles, and decisions to be made. But how well will they get done? That depends on you. It is simply impossible to overplan a wedding. No matter how many notes you take, contracts you sign, fittings you attend, and cakes you taste, something won't happen as you had planned. It's part of getting married. The snags are the things you will laugh about later. The things that went along perfectly are what you and your guests will cherish and remember most.

Give yourself as many wonderful memories as possible. Plan your wedding every step of the way. It will take time and effort but it will be fun, too.

Planning your wedding will bring you into the worlds of etiquette, food, fashions, furnishings, and feelings. Each will have its own challenges and rewards. You won't have to face them alone. Your fiancé will be there along with your parents, relatives, and friends. Everyone loves to offer opinions and ideas when it comes to weddings, because everyone loves weddings.

Keep your head, hold his hand, and follow your heart. That's the best advice for the months of planning ahead. It's all going to happen, and no matter what, these times will never come again.

Plan your wedding with ease and excitement. It will probably be easier than you think. Enjoy!

I N T R O D U C T I O N

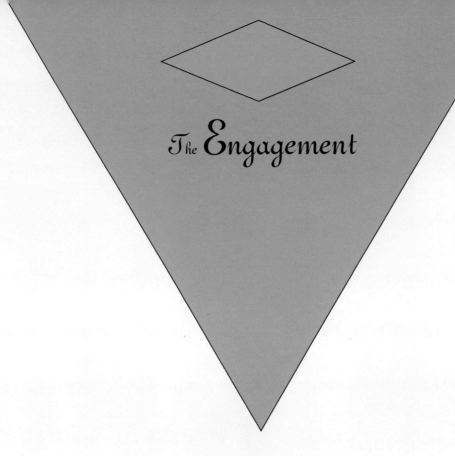

The Engagement

The important question *"Will you marry me?" can lead* to a plethora of social wills and won'ts, do's and don'ts. If you're getting married, both tradition and personal preferences are issues you will have to consider before that important day leading to a happily-ever-after life.

Step one usually revolves around the engagement ring. If the classic storybook romance is your ideal, chances are the third finger of your left hand will soon sparkle with a diamond solitaire ring. It's a tradition followed by 82 percent of all couples in America, Europe,

and Australia. You simply can't get more traditional than using a diamond ring to serve as the worldly symbol of your intentions to wed. This custom can be traced to the first official engagement ring known to modern history— a simple diamond solitaire set in a gold band presented by Archduke Maximilian of Austria to Mary of Burgundy on August 17, 1477. When he slipped that jeweled band on her finger, history was made, and the story continues with just about every engaged couple to this day …but with modifications.

C H A P T E R 1

© J. Taposchaner/FPG International

Because of its sparkle and purity of color, the diamond is the most popular choice of stone for an engagement ring. While a diamond may be a diamond, not all diamonds are equal in quality—or value. Knowing the four "Cs" of diamonds—carat, color, clarity, and cut—can help you "see" your way to a sound investment. If a diamond is not your ideal gem, choose something else. Princess Diana wears a sapphire and Princess Sarah sports a ruby, but whatever stone you want is the best choice of all.

Only about a third of marriage-minded men select and buy the engagement ring alone. He may know he wants to get married, but isn't sure about your ring size and taste in jewelry.

To accommodate your preferences, most reputable jewelers will sell engagement rings unseen by you under liberal conditions. Most often, these include allowing a full refund if the ring is returned within ten days, or an exchange in which the full purchase price of the first ring will be applied to the purchase of another—when you are there to make the final selection. The most reliable jewelers will also offer free engraving (for sentimental as well as identification purposes), and sizing to make sure the ring fits just right.

DIAMONDS

While most engaged couples select a diamond, beware and be wise. All diamonds are not equal—no matter how they may look to the untrained eye.

When it comes to diamonds, the evaluation involves four Cs: carat, color, clarity, and cut.

Carat weight, or size, is the most common starting point when it comes to purchasing a diamond. It's the easiest to see. The term "carat" as a unit of weight is derived from carob seeds used to balance scales in ancient times. A carat is equal to 200 milligrams. There are 142 carats to an ounce. Carats are further subdivided into points. There are 100 points to a carat. For example, if you are looking at a forty-five point carat (or .45) diamond, the stone weighs a little less than half a carat, which would be a fifty point (.50) stone. Because larger diamonds are quite rare, they have a greater value per carat.

"C" number two is color. All diamonds are white, right? Wrong. Diamonds come in a rainbow of colors—including red, yellow, green, blue, pink, and brown! These may be rare, but they do exist. But for all intents and purposes, white is the choice of most marriage-minded couples. But there are many variations among "white" diamonds alone.

A stone is graded for color from the whitest possible to the darkest known to man. Completely colorless, icy-white diamonds are rare…and valuable. Don't be fooled. What the jeweler says is "perfect" probably isn't, but that's only because "perfect" is near impossible to find. The same can be said for "blue-white" diamonds—white diamonds with a tinge of blue. These are the rarest of all diamonds, and most likely are impossible to find at a traditional jewelry store, unless the jeweler is a gemologist who specializes in such rare stones.

White diamonds are valued for their lack of color. The clearer the diamond, the higher the cost. "Color" in diamonds doesn't necessarily mean the stone has a dash of red, green, or blue running through it, but rather the effect of the absorption of certain parts of light. The whiter the diamond is, the more light passes through it, as opposed to one with a hint of color.

Clarity is the third "C" of diamond buying. A diamond's clarity is determined by taking into account the number, size, placement, color, and nature of any internal "inclusions" or external surface irregularities. Inclusions are imperfections caused by nature. These can be spots, bubbles, or lines formed in the stone when it was crystallized from carbon millions of years ago. These marks make each stone unique, as no two diamonds are identical.

When inclusions do not interfere materially with the passage of light through the stone, they do not affect its beauty. However, the fewer the inclusions, the more valuable the diamond. In the United States, Federal Trade Commission rules state that a diamond can be deemed "flawless" only when no imperfections can be seen by a trained eye looking through a ten-power magnifying glass in good light. The Gemological Institute of America uses a quality-analysis system that is most widely accepted for grading gemstones in the United States. Clarity is graded according to the relative position of the diamond on the F (flawless) to I (imperfect) scale.

Without any training or special magnification equipment, you can easily judge the fourth "C" of diamond selecting: cut. What you see is what you get. Diamonds are cut according to an exact mathematical formula. A finished diamond has fifty-eight facets. These are small, flat, polished planes cut to give the stone the maximum amount of light to reflect back into the viewer's eye. The reflection is called "brilliance" and is extremely important in evaluating the quality of a diamond. The widest circumference of a diamond is the "girdle." Above the girdle are thirty-two facets plus the "table," the largest and uppermost facet. Below the girdle are twenty-four facets plus the "cutlet," or point.

"Cut" also refers to the shape of the diamond. The most popular shapes are round, emerald (or rectangular), marquise (pointed on both ends), pear, oval, and heart. What shape stone looks best? Fashion experts say it is important to select a ring with the same attention as other jewelry, taking care to choose a ring that flatters the hand.

The length of the fingers is the determining factor. If you have long fingers, you can handle just about any style, but in all cases, rings must be selected in proportion to the size of the hand. If your long-fingered hands are also overly thin, oval or round settings are best because they soften the look. Also, wider bands are more flattering than thin ones.

If you have short fingers, you'll look best with a setting that remains within the knuckle. The setting or stone that extends past the knuckle will only accentuate your hand's shortness and make it look less elegant. Oval- or marquise-shaped stones elongate the hand and make a good choice if you have short fingers. The round solitaire setting is also good because of its simplicity. If you have a short hand but still want a large stone, a dome shape in a high setting will work best.

Whatever the shape or size of the ring, you should keep comfort in mind. Your hand is a working, functioning body area. Your finger and hand should move freely when decorated with the ring. That's what fashion experts have to say, but the ultimate decision is yours: Whatever you prefer is the best choice.

Colored Gemstones

Individual preferences are also the most important factor in selecting other stones as well. Just because most couples select a diamond engagement ring, it doesn't mean you must follow that tradition.

© Montes De Oca/FPG International

It's becoming more and more fashionable to wear a colored gemstone as an engagement ring, one that can be used with or without diamond accessories. Women with sophisticated tastes have taken a liking to colored gems and have made them just as "correct" as any diamond solitaire.

Despite Maximilian and Mary's noble heritage, colored gemstone engagement rings are the favorites among today's royalty. Princess Diana's engagement ring was a sapphire, while the Duchess of York opted for a ruby.

In addition to being "different," the colored gemstone engagement ring can also represent special meanings and desires. The "precious" colored stones are emeralds, rubies, and sapphires. These share the class with diamonds because they exhibit a phenomenal degree of rarity, beauty, and color—qualities a mineral must have in order to be termed a "gemstone."

Gemstones are beautiful, durable, rare…and retain their value.

A colored stone may also be selected to comply with your favorite or "lucky" color. Again, the best choice is what you like best.

Practical Considerations

Whether the stone is a diamond or zircon, there are two other "C's" to keep in mind: cost and care.

How much should an engagement ring cost? Only your budget can set the limits. According to statistics, the average diamond engagement ring costs $1,300, but a good rule of thumb when buying an engagement ring is to set aside two month's salary of one person. Remember, this is a once-in-a-lifetime purchase. Think of it as an investment that will endure forever.

The two months' salary rule will get you the biggest and best diamond your budget can probably afford, but as with every rule, there are exceptions. The diamond you can best afford now can always be "traded up" later, or "dressed up" with other rings, enhancers, or a different setting.

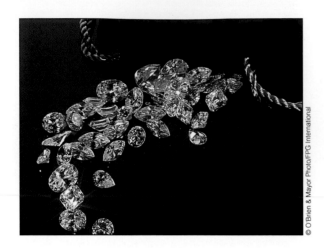

© O'Brien & Mayor Photo/FPG International

The Lore of Gems

The folklore behind a colored stone might determine your choice of engagement ring. According to tradition:

- **The blue aquamarine is thought to help establish happy marriages, as it reconciles the partners' differences.**
- **The green emerald signifies honesty and intelligence.**
- **The red ruby is said to ward off evil spirits and demonstrates clarity of the heart.**
- **The blue sapphire signifies faithfulness.**

The colored stone may also be chosen to signify your birthstone. The most accepted birthstone list is:

January—garnet
February—amethyst
March—aquamarine
April—diamond
May—emerald
June—pearl
July—ruby
August—peridot
September—sapphire
October—opal
November—yellow topaz
December—turquoise

Care of your gem is more important than words can ever say. The hardness of a diamond makes it the easiest stone to clean—and keep clean. The best method is with a jeweler's polishing cloth. Keep the diamond away from other gems. Because it is so hard, it can easily scratch your other jewelry. Diamonds can also scratch each other.

If the diamond gets smudged, soiled, or dusty, dip it in a commercial jewelry cleaner or a mix of ammonia and water. Scrub gently with a soft brush, rinse in clear water, and dry with a lint-free cloth. It should sparkle like new! Your jeweler probably has an ultrasonic cleaner. That's a quick way of giving your ring a first-class finish, too.

Don't wear your diamond while doing rough work. Even though the diamond is very hard, it has edges that can be chipped easily. Also, don't let your diamond come in contact with chlorine bleach. This can pit the stone and discolor the mounting.

Since colored gems are softer than diamonds, they require more care. For best results, clean your colored gemstone with a soft cloth and apply all colognes and toiletries before putting it on. The alcohol of a perfume or cream content of a lotion can cause permanent damage to the color of the stone.

Whether your engagement ring is the smallest diamond or the largest crown jewel, it's best to bring it to a jeweler once a year to be checked for loose prongs and wear of mountings. That's also the perfect opportunity for a professional shine.

ANNOUNCING THE ENGAGEMENT

The ring has been placed on your finger. Now what? Tell the world! It may be customary in your family or community for the groom-to-be to first ask permission from your father or parents before any announcement can be made. If such is the case, honor it. It's a moment you'll never regret.

If "permission" is not necessary, then the traditional way to spread the good news is first to your parents, then the groom's, and then close relatives and friends. If you want to be ultratraditional, you might only announce the engagement to your parents and let them in turn tell the world.

It is still customary, however, for your parents to make the formal announcement in the newspaper, but even that has undergone changes over the years as families have been reshuffled.

Engagement Etiquette

There may be definite social rules as to whom should make the engagement announcement, but when it comes to an engagement party, anyone can play host or hostess.

Traditionally, the bride's parents play host first to the groom's parents and then hold a party for all their friends and relatives. Once that honor has been given, and traditions followed, it's an open field for any and all parties.

Are engagement gifts necessary? Not really, although they have become customary. As the invitation's recipient is the guest of a person other than the couple, the guest can bring something for the host or hostess (such as flowers or a bottle of wine) and, if so desired, something for the couple (a small token of good luck, such as a gift certificate or cash).

Don't expect to be given anything substantial for an engagement party as there will be many other occasions in the near future at which gift-giving is more customary. Once you have registered your gift preferences and tableware patterns with a store, or made your color and gift selections known to a few relatives, an engagement gift can be sent to your home any time prior to the wedding.

Although you will thank the giver of each engagement gift in person, written thank-you notes should be sent within two weeks of presentation. Any longer will make the gesture seem like an afterthought.

Engagement gifts are given for your home with expected use after the wedding…not before, and not by either of your parents. As such, if the engagement is broken for any reason, all gifts should be returned to the givers within two weeks. This includes cash, checks, and all else, with the

For Example:

Should you have the traditional situation of parents married to each other, the official announcement might read:

"Mr. and Mrs. John Smith announce the engagement of their daughter Mary Anne to Mr. Joseph Jones."

This could be followed by the names of your fiancé's parents, and the couple's educational and professional backgrounds, and future wedding plans.

If your parents are divorced and not remarried, the first line of the announcement could read:

"Mr. John Smith and Mrs. Helen Smith announce...."

The same wording would apply if your parents are divorced and only your father has remarried.

If your parents are divorced and your mother has remarried, the announcement might read:

"Mr. John Smith and Mrs. Helen Smith White announce the engagement of their daughter...."

If your parents are no longer married as a result of death or divorce, and you were raised by your mother and stepfather, the announcement could begin:

"Mr. and Mrs. Walter White announce the engagement of Mary Anne Smith...."

(continued next page, first column)

The same wording could apply if your father and stepmother are making the announcement. Remember, the announcement needn't spell everything out and is certainly not the place to make private matters public.

Should your parents not be able to make the official announcement, it can be made by anyone, but it is usually reserved for a family member such as grandparents or a special relative. Examples:

"Mr. and Mrs. John Smith announce the engagement of their granddaughter Mary Anne Smith...."

"Mr. Andrew Black announces the engagement of his niece Mary Anne Smith...."

You and your fiancé can also announce your own engagement. The wording could read:

"Mary Anne Smith and Joseph Jones announce their engagement..."

Only under extremely rare situations should the groom's parents make the engagement announcement. Such situations occur only if he is of royal stature, such as when HRH Queen Elizabeth and Prince Philip announced their sons' engagements.

exceptions of fresh flowers and consumables, such as champagne or baskets of fruit.

How long should an engagement last? There really is no set answer. However, in the United States, the average engagement for a first-time marriage is nine months.

Often, financial, social, or other requirements may demand a longer engagement. For example, while you may plan on a six-month engagement, one

of you may be called to serve in national defense, thus forcing the engagement to be extended for a year or more. If you need time to save money for your new household, or the wedding's host needs time to become financially stronger, an engagement of a year or more may be necessary.

In major cities, the length of the engagement may be dictated by the amount of time the couple has to spend on the ceremony or reception site's "waiting list," which can sometimes be as much as eighteen months!

Religion can also dictate the length of an engagement period. A certain church or religion may require a couple to take a year of premarriage classes before the ceremony can be performed. It's also possible that in a marriage that will involve two religions, one member chooses to convert to the religion of the other, thus also extending an engagement period.

Should your engagement be broken, do not announce it in the newspapers, unless you or your fiancé is of very prominent social standing, such as royalty or the head of a government. The announcement is usually spread via word of mouth and writing when the gifts are returned. No reason has to be stated. A simple statement of "Mary Anne Smith and Joseph Jones have terminated their engagement for marriage" is sufficient. As those matters tend to be embarrassing for both parties, no details should be given…or expected.

Ending an engagement means more than just going your own way. Depending on the length of time you were engaged—and investments made for the wedding—ending an engagement can be a long and costly matter.

If the groom-to-be breaks the engagement, he must reimburse your parents for any deposits made to caterers, banquet halls, florists, photographers, and any other costs they may have incurred to assure services or products for the day of the proposed wedding.

Bridesmaids are to be reimbursed for any expenses incurred in buying their dresses. You, too,

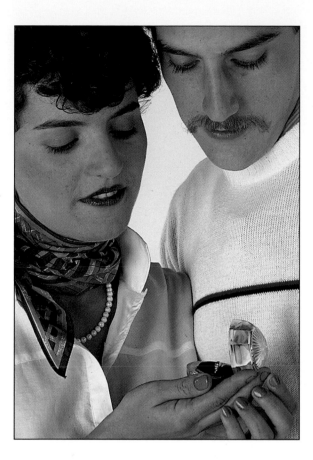

may ask for reimbursement if you had already made a deposit on a wedding gown.

Should you break the engagement, your parents do not necessarily receive reimbursements for expenses unless they choose to, however bridesmaids should be reimbursed for any expenses incurred.

What happens to the ring? That's a question that can have many answers. If the ring was also given as a Christmas, birthday, or other special occasion gift, it remains your property, unless you elect to give it back. It is customary, however, for you to return the ring if you broke off the engagement.

If the ring was given strictly as a symbol of love, and not also as a special occasion gift, it should be returned under all circumstances. With today's penchant for legal ramifications, breaking an engagement can also leave the couple standing in court—facing a lawsuit! Legally speaking, breaking an engagement can be considered a breach of promise. Depending on the temper and circum-

stances of the situation, getting out of an engagement can be costly and time-consuming. But no matter what, it's still easier on the nerves, social standing, and pocketbook than a divorce.

Encore Engagements

Although rare, sometimes an engaged couple will call off the wedding plans and then get reengaged at a later date. When that happens, it is done without much fanfare. No second announcement is put in the newspapers, nor should any of the other trappings that occurred before be repeated. Word of mouth will spread the message.

The topic of divorce also comes into play when one party is remarrying. Should it be the groom's second or subsequent marriage, socially speaking it makes no difference; the bride's circumstances set the tone of the engagement…and wedding.

With so many people divorcing today, getting remarried doesn't have the same social stigma it did even up to five years ago. However, some mode of proper decorum should still be followed. A new engagement is a new beginning. It's a new wedding being planned, not the fact that you are getting married again. Should it be your second engagement due to a divorce, an engagement ring is entirely proper. Since you are divorced anyway, chances are you no longer wear the first engagement ring or want anything to do with it.

If you still own the first ring, it could be returned to your first husband, sold, given away, put aside for your children's future engagements, or reset in another piece of jewelry for a child from your previous marriage.

If you are a widow, you should still not want to wear the first engagement ring, as a new wedding—and new start—is being planned. In either case, the new engagement ring should be as different as possible from the first. If this ring too has a diamond, it's appropriate to use a different shape, stone, or setting. A more suitable choice, however, might be a birthstone or other colored gem.

THE WEDDING LOCATION
AND RECEPTION

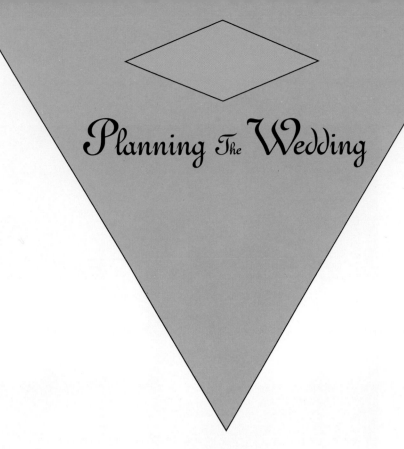

Planning The Wedding

In just about every area of life, there's a word that neatly sums up the secret to success. In real estate, it's "location, location, location." In comedy, it's "timing, timing, timing." When it comes to weddings, it's "planning, planning, planning." You simply cannot do too much planning. There are just too many parts to a wedding that need attention, and even in the best of circumstances one or two things might still be overlooked or underplanned. It simply can't be avoided. But those things won't spoil the day, either.

Start planning your wedding together on paper. You could use a notebook, a calendar, or simply a large piece of blank paper. List everything you think has to be accomplished in order to have the perfect wedding. Be sure you are both headed in the same direction. Then delegate who should do what and in what time frame. It may sound like a business deal at first, but you'll find this method not only saves each of you time and trouble but also demands that both parties take an equal role in planning the wedding.

C H A P T E R   2

The Wedding Location and Reception

There's a lot more to the wedding than just two people walking down an aisle and pledging their undying love. And even things as simple as those don't happen by chance. Depending on where you live and/or where you want the ceremony and reception, planning a wedding can take as short an amount of time as three months or as long as two years.

A common first step is to schedule a wedding date. For safety's sake, have a few dates in mind or a particular month or months. If you are planning a spring or summer wedding, you may have to allow yourself two years. As those times are the most popular for weddings, couples planning to get married then are often forced to plan well in advance to book the church or synagogue and/or reception location.

Decide what is more important to you, the place of the ceremony or the place of the reception. If you are planning a Catholic wedding, you may want to book the church first. Many Catholic churches require engaged couples to go through a series of lectures and classes, called Pre-Cana Conferences, before they can be married in a Catholic ceremony, let alone a nuptial mass.

A number of Christian religions will not permit wedding ceremonies in church during the holy seasons of Lent and Advent. Before you plan a Christmastime or late winter/early spring wedding, you should check with the minister about the church's regulations.

Be flexible about your date as well as ceremony time. Saturday afternoons are usually booked first. Next comes Saturday mornings, followed by Friday evenings and Sunday afternoons. If you can't get the time of the day you want, you may have to settle for either another time or date.

Once you have a ceremony time and place set, shop for a reception location. Some places will be booked as far as two years in advance, others no

Outdoor weddings continue to gain in popularity. They create a natural romantic atmosphere while accommodating an almost unlimited number of guests.

longer than one year. Don't be surprised if your first choice of reception location is booked solid as much as two years in advance. The banquet hall or restaurant also rents space to corporate parties, or holds private social functions, special civic events, and more. In short, your wedding reception may be special to you, but it can be a minor function to the caterer.

Should the reception location also serve as the site at which the ceremony will take place, you'll have two separate avenues of concern. Can the location handle both events? Will you be confined to one room or will the ceremony take place in an adjoining room? Is there a dressing room you and your attendants can use before the ceremony?

With rare exceptions, most reception locations that can also handle ceremonies will not have a judge, justice of the peace, or nondenominational minister on call to handle the official ceremony. You'll have to do this on your own. There are many types of people who are sanctioned by the government to officiate over a wedding. These range from judges to mayors to magistrates. Book one early, as schedules are filled quickly. Be careful, too. If you plan your wedding more than a year in advance, be sure that the judge, mayor, or whoever will still be in office at the time of your wedding. If there's an election taking place between the time you book the local mayor and the time of your wedding, you may be asking for trouble. Another point to keep in mind is the location of your reception. Be sure the civic official who you want to conduct your wedding has jurisdiction in that location—if not, the marriage will not be considered legally valid.

Depending on where you live, your country may require just a civil ceremony, but you may, for personal reasons, want a religious ceremony, too. These should take place within a day of each other—with the civil ceremony happening first. Good and early planning will make this possibility happen.

Ceremony Etiquette and Legalities

It is customary just to have the maid of honor and best man at the civil ceremony, but all family and friends at the religious one. Since that puts an extra burden on your maid of honor and best man, your planning should include their schedules. Will they be available for both ceremonies? If not, you can either change dates or have two sets of witnesses, but remember that under the law, the civil ceremony is the only one that counts. You are legally married when a government official pronounces you as such. Whoever signs the state's book as your witness will be considered your official maid of honor and best man. The book signing after the religious service is strictly for the church's records.

Health and money come into play in every aspect of the wedding. Whether your wedding is civil, religious, or both, you'll still have to abide by local governmental regulations concerning licenses and blood tests. These should be accomplished at least ten days prior to the wedding—two weeks will give you plenty of time.

About a month before the wedding, call the city hall or county services office within the jurisdiction of where your wedding is to take place. The county clerk, freeholder, or board of health official should be able to answer your questions about blood tests and license particulars. Be sure to ask about costs and processing time, as well as what identification you will need in order to get the license. Some states require no identification at all, allowing you to get married using any name or age you want. Others require you to marry only under your legal name and insist you use your official birth date. Some jurisdictions also require that two people unrelated to you vouch that you are who you claim to be and the age you claim to be. If the town where your wedding is taking place has such clauses, be sure to bring friends with you who can answer those questions. Should this be the second marriage for you or the groom, be sure to have the divorce, annulment, or certificate of death papers with you—whichever applies in your individual case. Claiming ignorance of legal paperwork, the need for witnesses, or any other issue at the time of filing for a marriage license will not help your cause or speed up the process.

Plan on being at the government building at least two hours just to file for a license and have any required blood tests taken. Both the health department and license bureau take care of more duties than weddings. Don't be surprised if the person standing ahead of you in the licensing line is there for a hunting permit—it's just the nature of the business.

Logistics

The ceremony, no matter where it will take place, will probably be the most trouble-free part of your wedding plans. The reception will be just the opposite. Here all the elements come into play. If you are not careful, you can get caught up in a web of unnecessary bothers. Be on guard for anything.

Outdoor weddings are picturesque and romantic, but also leave you at the mercy of the weather. If an outdoor wedding is your plan A, then be sure to have a plan B. Don't despair, however. Should the skies over your wedding location get dark and rainy or the temperature turn cold, beautiful tents complete with heaters can be set up within minutes. If the garden setting is not near a building that can serve as a quick indoor location, take the precaution and have a tent set up nearby. You'll find some guests will prefer sitting in the tent or under the canopy no matter how magnificent the outdoor setting. Better to be safe than sorry. Never leave yourself wide open for weather trouble. No matter what the weather forecast, sudden changes have been known to happen; so be prepared.

Should your wedding be indoors or out, be sure to provide the necessary amenities. These include enough private toilets and washing facilities to handle the crowd and enough parking within a reasonable walking distance of the reception site. Check into the safety of the parking area, too. Does the lot

Selecting Wedding Rings

Your wedding plans will run from the top of your head—as in the ideas in your mind—to the tip of your fingers, as in wedding rings. On the surface, selecting marriage bands may seem like the simplest of wedding-related tasks, but will probably end up being more complicated than you think.

Even before you set foot in a jewelry store to buy a ring, do some planning together. Questions the bride especially should think about include:

- Will the groom be wearing a wedding ring? Many men prefer not to. Others can't, due to safety precautions at work or an allergy to gold, especially yellow gold.

- Will you be wearing matching rings? If so, how will your ring work in conjunction with your wedding band?

- Will the ring be worn on the traditional third finger of the left hand or do you or your religion require the ring to be worn on another finger? In Orthodox Jewish weddings, the bride's ring is placed on her index finger. In some religions, the ring is worn on the middle finger.

- Does the ring you selected comply with religious customs? In traditional Jewish weddings, the rings cannot be adorned with stones. They must be of plain, solid gold. Often the Jewish couple will also buy jewel-encrusted rings to wear after the ceremony.

- Will the rings be engraved? If so, with what?

- What about insurance? Does your current homeowner's policy cover jewelry or do you need an additional rider?

- Are you prepared to pay for the rings? Tradition says the groom should pay for the bride's ring, and vice versa.

Once these questions have been answered, shop around for your wedding rings—and by all means try them on before you leave the store. Should you need to get them adjusted, make sure the sizing was done correctly at least a month in advance. Keeping them in the box until the ceremony and finding out then that the ring or rings weren't sized correctly will leave you in a very embarrassing situation.

There's an old saying that a gift sometimes means more to the giver than the receiver; such might be the case with wedding rings. Say you or the groom have wedding rings that have been in the family for years and have sentimental, if not monetary, value. If you would like to use them at your wedding, discuss the matter openly and candidly with your groom before it is too late to buy new rings. For example, your late grandfather may have meant the world to you and you would like your groom to wear your grandfather's wedding ring as his own. Should your groom prefer a new ring, don't get upset. Wear your grandfather's ring on a chain around your neck or keep it in your personal jewelry box for safe keeping, but don't expect your groom to have the same feelings for your relatives, dead or alive, that you do. He wasn't raised among them—you were. On the same token, the groom shouldn't expect you to wear his mother's or grandmother's wedding ring if you don't want to. Another alternative is to have the stone reset.

If you or the groom were married previously, never use the same wedding ring as before. That ring may be a symbol of your new love, but it is also a reminder of a painful time. Trade it in for a new ring. You won't regret it.

With no visible beginning or end and made of the most precious commodity, the ring of gold is an international symbol of eternal love. As your most important and constantly worn piece of jewelry, be sure your ring is comfortable and suitable to your lifestyle. Choose a ring that will not interfere with your normal everyday activities. Other things to consider: Is there a companion ring for the groom? Does your religion have requirements regarding the ring? Can the ring be sized and engraved in time for the wedding?

or parking area have enough security so all the cars will be free from harm or theft while guests enjoy your wedding? Vandals know the owners of those cars will be occupied during your wedding. That gives them plenty of time to steal or ransack even the most secure car. Make sure you provide proper parking security for your guests.

Do your family and friends like to dance? If so, be sure the location has an ample dance floor and sound system. Even outdoors, this is possible by adding a low stage area under the tent. Also make sure that all the guests have easy access to the bar and dance floor and that there is enough room to circulate easily between tables. If the wedding is indoors, also consider emergency exits. Are there enough and are they in working order? Should any of your guests be unable to climb steps, does the location have a side ramp entrance? All points should be covered before you place any deposits.

Be sure too that wherever you decide to have your ceremony and/or reception stays within the framework of the type of wedding you want. For example, if you want a small, informal wedding, the chapel in the rectory might be more appropriate than use of a full church or cathedral. Any outdoor wedding, even in the most splendid garden, will still have an aura of informality. Plan your wedding style according to taste, budget, and the size of the guest list. This last point is very important. Unless your guest list is limited to fifty or under, your wedding is unlikely to be small and cozy. Although you may have always wanted a wedding to rival those held at Buckingham Palace, if you don't have the budget to match such ultraformality, then don't do it. You may feel like Princess Diana on your wedding day, but trying to conduct a wedding that is out of your budget range will just make you and your guests uncomfortable.

Family Considerations

A wedding may be the joining of two people, but it really involves more people than that. If your family is a big, happy one, count your blessings. You have a

rare situation. In today's society, many families have been fragmented through divorce, remarriages, separations, and the like. Should such be the case with either of your families, your task is more difficult.

Even if your family includes the worst of enemies, there's no reason why both parties can't at least be polite to each other for the few hours of your wedding. They should give you that much love and respect. However, make sure you don't force the issue by putting them together more often than absolutely necessary.

Be they divorced or separated, your parents are

your parents. Even if you are closer to one than the other, weddings have a way of making the blood connection stronger than ever. They also have a way of renewing the pain of hurt feelings. Be true to your parents, but also true to yourself. If you are closer to your stepfather than your biological father, then your stepfather should get the honors of walking you down the aisle, having the first dance, etc. Your biological father will be a guest. The reverse is true if you are closer to your stepmother than your biological mother.

Seating will be very important to them. It should

Dividing the Expenses

Tradition says the bride and her parents should pay for some parts of the wedding, and the groom and his parents should pay for others. These are only suggestions, however, not rules. It really doesn't matter who pays for what, but use some common sense. Under no circumstances should the bride pay for her own bouquet or wedding ring. The groom should at the very least pay for those—along with the license. On the other hand, the bride should always pay for the groom's wedding ring.

Going strictly by the book, the following lists of wedding expense responsibilities apply. Don't hesitate, however, to redivide the expenses to suit your situation:

Bride pays for:
- Groom's ring
- Wedding gift for groom
- Gifts for female attendants
- Groom's boutonniere
- Blood test and medical examination

Groom pays for:
- Bride's engagement and wedding rings
- Wedding gift for bride

- Gifts for male attendants
- Flowers for bride and the mothers and boutonnieres for men in wedding party
- Marriage license
- Bachelor dinner
- Fee for minister and all other ceremony-related expenses, such as the organist, soloist, altar servers, etc.
- All honeymoon expenses

Jointly, the bride and groom can pay for:
- Personal stationery
- Honeymoon expenses
- Photographer
- Gifts for attendants

Bride's family pays for:
- Bride's wedding clothing
- Wedding stationery, such as announcements and invitations
- All wedding photography
- Flowers for the ceremony, reception, and bridesmaids
- Transportation for the wedding party
- Reception

Groom's parents pay for:
- Rehearsal dinner

not be a problem to you. At the ceremony, whatever parent you are closest to, and their current spouse or significant other, should sit in the first row or pew. The other parent and current mate should sit in the second row or pew. At the reception, put them at separate tables along with close relatives. Photographs are also no problem. Everyone can be in the same photo but on different sides of you. You'll find that distance is the best deterrent to trouble. If anyone should start acting up by dwelling on old problems, politely ask them to let you please have this one day full of happiness and cooperation. They should behave accordingly.

If you think tempers could easily flare, ask an usher to be on guard to serve as referee. You may also want to give that trusted friend-usher hints on other people who for various reasons should be watched. These might include an uncle who has a drinking problem, an especially shy aunt who likes to dance but needs coaxing, etc.

Children in the Ceremony

History shows that children were first used in wedding ceremonies to ensure a bride's fertility. Today they are just cute additions. Formal weddings tend not to have children in the bridal party. But more family-oriented events, and second marriages, sometimes include them.

Children can be a lovely or trying part of the wedding. This is a clear matter of when in doubt, don't! For safety's sake, don't ask any child under the age of seven to be the flower girl or ring bearer—then only the most mature ones at that. A four-year-old niece who may be delightful at home can quickly become fearful when facing a room full of strangers. The ceremony may be only an hour, but to a frisky five-year-old it can seem like a day and a half. Children are children—even when dressed up as little adults.

In any event, children probably will be most comfortable sitting with their parents rather than being on stage with you.

Planning Timetable

Here are some planning guidelines for you.

Bride's List

At least six months prior to the wedding:

- Select wedding date (with groom)
- Reserve locations for ceremony and reception
- Select female attendants
- Work on preliminary budget with parents and groom
- Begin compiling guest list
- Select gown, photographer, florist, caterer, and other services
- Announce engagement in the newspaper
- Register gift preferences at a local store
- Shop for trousseau
- Plan honeymoon (with groom)
- Book officiant for the wedding
- Hire wedding consultant (if so desired)
- Keep your sense of humor

Four to six months prior to the wedding:

- Complete guest list
- Complete wedding reception details; make deposits and sign contracts
- Complete ceremony details. Attend any prenuptial classes the officiant may require
- Have both mothers coordinate and select their dresses
- Complete orders for wedding clothing
- Order wedding stationery
- Shop for wedding rings (with groom)
- Complete gift registry list
- Hold dinner party for both sets of parents
- Introduce members of wedding party to each other

Two to four months prior to the wedding:

- Purchase wedding rings
- Purchase gifts for attendants and your parents

- Address wedding invitations and announcements
- Plan luncheon for attendants

One to two months prior to the wedding:

- Start working on seating arrangements
- Plan your pre-wedding portraits (with photographer)
- File for marriage license and get blood tests
- Have final fittings for wedding clothing
- Keep notes of gifts received
- Send thank-you notes for shower gifts
- Complete all accessory purchases, such as garter, gloves, jewelry, etc.
- Have an attorney review any prenuptial agreements

Three weeks prior to the wedding:

- Mail all wedding invitations
- Finalize all plans with florist, caterer, and other service people
- Assign duties to friends and relatives concerning housing for out-of-town guests, transportation, safety, etc.
- Hold luncheon for your attendants, and present them with their gifts. Give gifts to fiancé and parents
- Select wedding portrait for newspaper announcement
- Address announcements to be mailed out after the wedding
- Make appointment with hairdresser and manicurist
- Have your wedding gown pressed and delivered to your home
- File change-of-name and address forms with the post office and your company's personnel office (if applicable)
- Change beneficiaries on yours and the groom's insurance policies

- Pick up wedding rings. Be sure they are properly sized and engraved
- Complete all religious, legal, and medical paperwork to reflect married status; this is especially important if you are going to change your name so the new identifications will be waiting for you after the honeymoon

Two weeks prior to the wedding:

- Complete seating arrangements for ceremony and reception (with groom)
- Confirm all honeymoon arrangements
- Secure marriage license (with groom)
- Work out gift delivery schedule with store where you registered
- Send in newspaper announcement. Be sure it has a release date

One week prior to the wedding:

- Write as many thank-you notes as you can to those who have sent wedding gifts
- Try on all wedding and honeymoon clothes for last-minute alterations
- Pack for honeymoon
- Attend rehearsal and dinner
- Get plenty of rest

Wedding Day:

- Have a good breakfast
- Have hair, nails, and makeup done
- Have all clothing and accessories ready to be put on at least two hours in advance
- Attendants should be at designated meeting point at least an hour before the ceremony
- Arrive at ceremony location at least twenty minutes before the wedding is to start
- Be sure going away outfit is waiting at reception site
- Assign an attendant to take care of your wedding gown
- Enjoy your wedding day. There's nothing else you can do now!

After the wedding:

- Send out remaining thank-you notes
- Select your wedding photos
- Mail announcements
- Entertain your wedding party, parents, and anyone else who was a big help
- Live happily ever after

Groom's List

At least six months prior to the wedding:

- Begin compiling guest list
- Select male attendants
- Plan honeymoon (with bride)
- Work on preliminary budget (with bride)
- Register gift selections (with bride)
- Keep your sense of humor

Four to six months prior to the wedding:

- Complete your guest list. Ask your parents to do the same and give list to bride
- Shop for wedding rings (with bride)
- Look into license and health certificate requirements
- Attend any necessary prenuptial classes
- Make deposit for honeymoon
- Start shopping for wedding clothes

Two to four months prior to the wedding:

- Purchase wedding rings
- Purchase gifts for attendants and parents
- Arrange rehearsal dinner with your parents
- Help out-of-town guests and relatives with their travel plans

One to two months prior to the wedding:

- Help bride with reception seating arrangements
- File for marriage license and get blood tests
- Complete all necessary honeymoon clothing and accessory purchases
- Order wedding clothing. Be sure all attendants have done the same

- Order bride's bouquet and mothers' corsages
- If applicable, have attorney prepare prenuptial agreement
- Complete rehearsal dinner plans
- Book makeup artist, manicurist, hair stylist for wedding day, if so desired

Three weeks prior to the wedding:

- Change beneficiaries on yours and the bride's insurance policies
- Hold party for your attendants
- Assign duties to best man and head usher
- Finalize all housing plans for out-of-town guests
- Pick up wedding rings. Make sure they are sized and engraved properly
- Complete all legal, medical, and religious paperwork to reflect newly married status

Two weeks prior to the wedding:

- Complete seating arrangements (with bride)
- Confirm all honeymoon arrangements
- Secure marriage license (with bride)
- Have final fittings on wedding clothing
- Arrange transportation for wedding party— including yourself
- Send flowers to your fiancée. She's going through some trying times right now

One week prior to the wedding:

- Confirm appointment with hair stylist, etc.
- Have car tuned up, cleaned, etc.
- Arrange transportation to and from the airport or train station in conjunction with your honeymoon trip

- Pick up wedding clothing and try on. Have last-minute alterations made
- Give attendants and parents their gifts
- Give bride her wedding gift
- Pack for honeymoon
- Notify post office of your new address

- Pay for bride's bouquet and mothers' corsages
- Pay for boutonnieres
- Attend rehearsal
- Get plenty of rest

Wedding Day:

- Have a good breakfast
- Have hair groomed
- Have florist deliver bride's bouquet and corsages to mothers three hours prior to the wedding
- Be sure all clothing is laid out at least two hours before ceremony
- Be sure ushers are at church at least an hour before ceremony
- Have best man help you dress for wedding and drive you to the church at least thirty minutes before ceremony
- Be sure you have all honeymoon tickets, money, etc. in a safe place
- Be sure all attendants—and yourself—have the right boutonnieres
- Give best man sealed envelopes holding the fee for clergy and other ceremony associates
- Be sure best man has marriage license with him so it can be signed by everyone after the ceremony
- Be sure change of clothing is at reception
- Designate an attendant to be sure your tuxedo is returned to the rental place
- Enjoy yourself

After the wedding:

- Send thank-you note and gift to bride's parents for the wonderful wedding
- Invite wedding party and parents to your new home
- Select wedding pictures
- Live happily ever after

STYLES AND
POSSIBILITIES
THE GUEST LIST

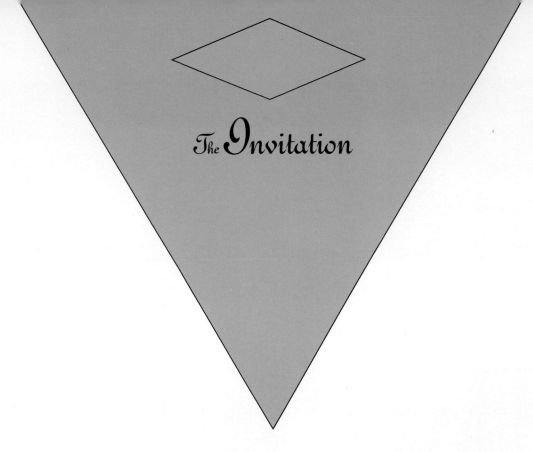

The Invitation

*O*nce upon a time, wedding invitations were either white cards with black block lettering or ivory cards with black script lettering. Every wedding invitation basically looked the same as the one before it and after it. Only the names, times, places, and dates were changed. Then came the color revolution.

Almost overnight, wedding invitations went from ordinary to original. Invitations were suddenly available in every color, shape, size, and form imaginable. Some even rivaled circus posters! Both extremes are now over.

Contemporary wedding invitations come in as many colors, sizes, and styles as you could ever want. We now have available the combination of high-quality paper and sophisticated printing processes. As a result, your invitation can be as formal and elegant or casual as you like.

Visit a few stores or companies that specialize in wedding stationery. Each will have a rainbow of possibilities from which to choose. If you don't find exactly what you want, visit a printer who can help you design your own invitations and have them done at an affordable price.

C H A P T E R 3

Judith and Leon Morrow
would be honored
by your presence
at the marriage of their daughter

Elena Janice Morrow
to
Theodore Alexander Spitzer

Sunday, October 7,
The Palm House
Brooklyn Botanic Garden
Brooklyn, New York

Ceremony at six o'clock

Reception following

© Christopher C. Bain

The invitation sets the tone of the entire wedding.

STYLES AND POSSIBILITIES

The invitation should be as formal or informal as the wedding. After all, it will reflect the tone for the entire affair, as it is the first exposure your guests will have to what's ahead.

If it's your first wedding, chances are you'll want the most traditional invitation possible. That's perfectly alright. While you're at it, select coordinating reception cards, announcements, "at-home" cards, and informals (monogrammed notecards on which you write your own message). All will soon come in handy. The more items you order at the same time—and on the same kind of paper—the better the deal the printer will be able to offer.

Invitations are just that: your way to invite people to attend your wedding ceremony. These are mailed three to four weeks prior to the wedding. The complete invitation consists of the invitation card and two envelopes. The first envelope (without the gummed edge) holds the invitation and is addressed to just the names of the people who are invited, such as, Mr. and Mrs. John Smith. If the couple has children

under the age of eighteen who are also invited to the wedding, the envelope would be addressed, Mr. and Mrs. John Smith, Master John Smith, Jr., Miss Susan Smith. Children over the age of eighteen should receive their own invitations.

The ungummed envelope (with the invitation inside) is enclosed in the envelope with a gummed edge, on which the entire mailing address would be written. At one time, it was necessary to put a piece of tissue paper on the invitation prior to putting it into an envelope. That was to blot any ink that may not have dried by the time the invitation was addressed. Modern printing methods have eliminated such worry. But, if you like the look of a piece of tissue for formality reasons, your printer should be able to provide it at little, if any, cost.

When stuffing envelopes, the inside envelope is faced toward the back of the outer envelope, so that when it is opened, the first writings seen are the names of the invited guests.

For the people invited to the ceremony who are also coming to the reception, a reception card should be enclosed with the invitation. It simply gives the details of the reception: Time, place, and, if necessary, phone number or address to which invitees should respond to notify their acceptance or rejection of the invitation.

A fairly modern invention is the Rsvp card which the invitee is expected to complete and mail back to the wedding's hosts to notify them if the prospective guests will or will not attend the reception. Purists think such reply cards are in bad taste, but modern social conditions have forced the issue.

With the art of letter-writing having fallen out of fashion, many people have no idea how to properly respond to the letter's Rsvp (which represents the French words for "respond if you please"). To save embarrassment to guests and unexpected expenses to hosts, the cards have become a "must" ingredient to every wedding invitation.

Another addition to the invitation can be an at-home card. This notifies guests of your new address and the date you will start receiving company. Due to modern social customs, the at-home card is also a clear way of telling everyone if the bride will retain her maiden name.

THE GUEST LIST

Once all the particulars of wording have been worked out, you'll have a colorful task: creating your guest list. That's strictly up to the couple and both sets of parents. Your budget and the size of the reception location can only handle so many people. Make a list that abides by those restrictions.

Divide the number of available places so that all parties (the couple, their parents) are able to first invite everyone who "must" be invited, and then whomever they would also like to invite. Priority is always given to the host and hostess' list. They divide the number of invitations as to how they feel best, too.

If you disagree with the number of invitations your parents gave you, you could always host your own wedding reception or host a big open-house party for all your friends soon after you return from your honeymoon.

At-Home Card Examples

If you are going to take on the title of "Mrs.," the at-home card would read:

Mr. and Mrs. Walter Frederick White
at home after September 3
1234 Apple Lane
Hometown, Wyoming, zip code
Phone number

Should the bride decide to retain her maiden name, the first line would read: Sally Smith and Walter Frederick White. The rest would be the same.

Should the groom's parents want to invite more people than the bride's parents can afford, it would not be improper for them to offer to pay for the cost of providing dinner for the extras. It is also not improper for the groom's parents to hold a party in honor of the couple shortly after their honeymoon.

Extended family members and friends know that

there are budget and size restrictions on every wedding. Any hurt feelings will quickly heal with an invitation to a post-wedding open-house party. Handwritten invitations—on your informals—are perfectly acceptable.

Chances are both you and your fiancé are employed and have many business acquaintances who might be a big part of your professional life but matter little on your personal side. There is no need to invite them to your wedding. Your wedding is not a business function. You can always entertain those people later in your home.

Making up the invitation list will be a trying task. Feelings are bound to be hurt—there's no getting around it. Chances are no bride since the beginning of time ever invited everyone who should, could, or wanted to be invited. You won't be the exception to the rule.

The cost of food and beverages, or wishes for formality, have caused many a bride and groom to curtail their lists and limit the guests to adults only. That is, no children under eighteen are welcome to the

ceremony or reception. If your wedding falls under that category, do not make mention of the fact on the invitation. There is no place on the invitation for such a social remark. You can clearly make your feelings known on the inside envelope, where you list only the names of those invited to the affair. If a guest makes mention of a child on the Rsvp, it is up to your parents, or whoever else is hosting the event, to make the phone call and express in kind terms that the children are not invited to the affair.

The invitation is also not the place to make requests for special gifts such as cash. If you are strapped for funds, or feel another silver bowl would be one too many, let the wedding's host gently get the word out. When and if a guest should call for a gift suggestion, the host could say that you and your fiancé already have a completely furnished home, but are saving for a special trip or purchase. The guest should get the message.

If for any reason the wedding should be postponed or canceled after the invitations are mailed, it is up to the host to contact each guest by phone or informal note about the situation. No great details are needed, simply a message reading: The impending marriage of our daughter Sally to Walter White has been cancelled. Thank you for your understanding. Sincerely, John and Helen Smith.

Other Considerations

The informals you ordered with your invitations will serve as thank-you notes, plus be used as standard informals after that task has been accomplished.

Purists believe that invitations and announcements must be addressed by hand, but modern calligraphy machines have eased that restriction, giving you an option. However, there is no option when it comes to sending out written thank-you notes. Preprinted notes are totally unacceptable. It's disrespectful to your guests—and a very bad reflection on you—to use such stationery. (See Chapter 7, "Gifts," for a description of appropiate thank-you note wording.)

Announcement Examples

Announcements are just that: a means to announce to everyone who was not invited to the wedding but is interested that you were married. Announcements look very much like invitations, but with slightly different wording. Example:

Announcement:
Mr. and Mrs. John Smith
announce the marriage of
their daughter Sally Jane
to
Mr. Walter Frederick White
on Friday, the third of September
One thousand nine hundred and ninety-three
The Church of All Faiths
Hometown, Wyoming

Since the person to whom the announcement is addressed won't have to worry about attending the ceremony, there is no need to mention the time of the event nor the address of the location. Announcements are mailed the day after the wedding, and still use the double envelope. Announcements can also carry at-home cards; see box on page 30.

Unless your wedding is extremely large, or there are numerous special guests who may not be recognized on sight by the ushers, pew cards are not necessary. However, if your wedding conditions do fit those situations, your printer can provide you with pew cards. These are nothing more than simple white cards that are mailed with the invitation, on which is written the number of the pew you wish the guest to occupy. The guest hands the card to the usher upon reaching the church's door. The usher then follows the seating plan you created.

Wording the Invitation

With the current relaxed social conditions, an invitation can use one of many acceptable wordings. Here are a few suggestions, one of which should apply to your particular case:

If the bride's parents are married, the invitation could read:

Mr. and Mrs. John Smith
request the honor of your presence
at the marriage of their daughter
Sally Jane
to
Mr. Walter Frederick White
on Friday, the third of September
at six o'clock
The Church of All Faiths
Pine Road at Willow Lane
Hometown, Wyoming

If the bride's parents are divorced but her mother hasn't remarried, the first line of the invitation could read:

Mr. John Smith and Mrs. Helen Smith
request the honor of your presence
at the marriage of their daughter
Sally Jane

If the bride's parents are divorced and her mother has remarried, the invitation could read:

Mr. John Smith and
Mrs. Helen Smith Black
request the honor of your presence
at the marriage of their daughter
Sally Jane

© J.B. Fairfax Press

The wording of the invitation should be as formal or casual as the wedding itself.

If the bride's parents are divorced and both remarried, but the bride was raised by her mother and her new husband, and has no desire to give her father any special attention, the invitation could read:

Mr. and Mrs. Jason Green
request the honor of your presence
at the marriage of
Miss Sally Jane Smith

If a parent is deceased, the invitation could read:

Mrs. John Smith
requests the honor of your presence
at the marriage of her daughter
Sally Jane

As much as you might still love your deceased parent, he or she can no longer extend invitations and therefore is not mentioned on the stationery.

If your grandparents are hosting the event, the invitation could read:

Mr. and Mrs. Hugo Brown
request the honor of your presence
at the marriage of their granddaughter
Sally Jane

If friends are the hosts, the invitation could read:

Mr. and Mrs. William Blue
request the honor of your presence
at the marriage of
Miss Sally Jane Smith

If so desired, the couple can extend their own invitation. If that is the case, appropriate wording could be:

Miss Sally Jane Smith
and
Mr. Walter Frederick White
request the honor of your presence
at their marriage

Unless the groom's parents are hosting the wedding, which would be a very rare occasion, their names do not appear on the invitation, nor does their marital status affect the wording of the invitation.

PERSONAL SHOWER
STYLES

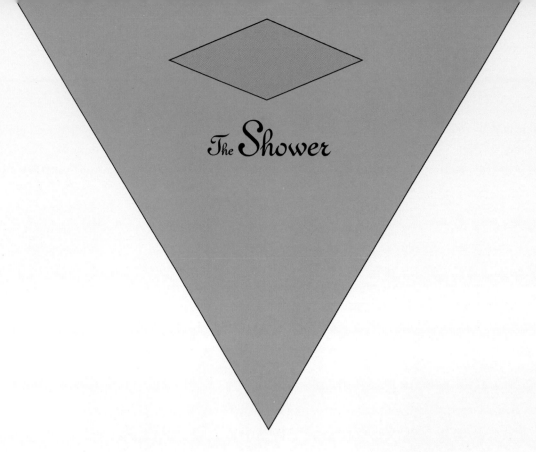

The Shower

"*Showering*" *the engaged couple with gifts has* become one of the happiest, most creative, and memorable of all premarriage rituals. While modern times have filled this custom with mirth, its roots can be traced to situations that were just the opposite.

An eighteenth-century tale from the Netherlands relates the story of the first wedding shower. It seems the bride's father didn't care for her choice of husband and refused to give her a dowry, thus eliminating any chance of her marrying at that time. To accomplish his mission of marriage, the prospective groom told the townsfolk of his plight. They joined forces and shared their wares and riches with the couple, thus "showering" the bride with enough of a dowry to make the marriage socially acceptable.

The other story about how the wedding shower originated stems from an equally old tale of how a poor girl in Europe fell in love with a young man above her social standing. His family wouldn't hear of the marriage due to the prospective bride's status. Word of her situation spread through town and people from far and near gathered together and "showered" gifts on the young woman until her financial standing was worthy of the young man's heart, in the eyes of his family.

Whether either of these stories is correct is neither here nor there. They do, however, share a common theme of friends expressing good wishes toward the engaged couple by giving them gifts.

PERSONAL SHOWER STYLES

In more recent history, the shower became the "bridal shower." This is an event where only the bride-to-be is surrounded with gift-bearing friends and family members. For many brides, that scenario still holds true, but its becoming more the exception

than the rule. Today's social and professional lifestyles are turning the traditional shower into a series of showers. Taking into account that the bride is likely to have both longtime, hometown friends as well as those from her professional circle, and that everyone may be scattered over long distances, the shower is taking on new meaning—and frequency.

On average, today's bride can expect to be honored at three such events. One might be a large event with her personal friends and family members in attendance. A smaller event could be held in conjunction with her professional life, and a third might take place when she visits the out-of-town location prior to the wedding.

Your situation may be totally different. It may involve only one shower, or as many as five. The

number isn't important, as they all serve the same purpose: an opportunity for those who care about you to share in your happiness. Because sharing has become the underlying theme of contemporary showers (as opposed to yesteryear's purpose of taking care of the bride's household needs), it's becoming more and more common for "bridal showers" to be "wedding showers," where the *couple* is honored, *not* just the future bride. This trend is expected to continue as the his/her social rules of old keep blending into one new set of standards.

Theme Showers

Because so many couples today have assembled more than enough housewares and appliances

---

Shower Invitations

The tone of the shower is set by whoever hosts it. If the shower is to be a large, formal affair, invitations can be as formal as those for the wedding. For example, a shower hosted by both the maid of honor and the best man could have invitations that read:

Sally Smith and John Jones
cordially invite you to a
wedding shower
in honor of
Betty Black and William White

This would be followed by the time, location, an Rsvp number, and theme, if any.

For a less formal shower, the invitations could be handwritten with simple, straightforward wording such as:

Please attend the bridal shower for
Betty Black

Shower Etiquette

No matter if the shower is for her, him, or them, certain guidelines are followed.

- The shower is never hosted by the bride-to-be's mother. Although the mother may have a hand in the planning, she is expected to be a guest at the affair. The shower is traditionally organized and presided over by the bride-to-be's friends and nonimmediate family members.

- If it is to be a "couples" shower, the groom's friends—not his immediate family members—may also do the planning and hosting.

- Once upon a time, the etiquette books said only women who would be invited to the wedding could be invited to the shower. Due to financial and geographical constraints, that rule has changed. General showers can be attended by any friends and relatives of the bride and/or groom. If the shower is one of a more specific nature, such as an office party or sorority event, then the invitee list would be for appropriate members only. The same rules apply if the shower is for him or the couple.

- The shower is always held four to six weeks prior to the wedding. Any closer to the wedding will interfere with the couple's nuptial planning calendar.

- The same guests are usually not invited to more than one shower, as it would be a strain on their budgets…and an embarrassment to the couple.

- Even if the shower itself is a surprise, there is no need to turn it into a party filled with novelty shop items. A shower should always be held in good taste. The purpose is to honor the couple and not embarrass them. There'll be plenty of time at the bachelor and bachelorette parties for the jokes!

before ever getting married, showers have become creativity sessions rather than events fulfilling needs. As a result, theme showers have become popular. Set by the host or hostess, the theme can be anything from decorating a room in the house to doting on the couple's hobbies to catering to their wildest fantasies. The tone of the theme is often set by that of the shower itself. If the shower is just to honor the bride or groom alone, a more intimate theme might come into play than one that would be enjoyed by mixed company.

If there's a theme or two that you and your groom find particularly appealing, drop hints to the maid of honor, best man, and close friends. For example, tell them how you read about a "bath-and-bedroom" theme and thought it was such a great idea. Here's a list of themes to give you inspiration:

- **A Room in the House.** Every guest is asked to bring an item that can be used in a specific room in the house. One guest might be asked to bring something for the bedroom, another the bathroom, another the living room, etc. This theme works especially well if the your selection of household colors and tastes is known.
- **Around-the-Clock.** Guests are asked to bring items that can be used at various times of the day. One invitation might read, "Please bring something the couple can use during the first hour of the day." (The possibilities can be bath products, bed linens, breakfast equipment, etc.) Another might read, "Please bring something the couple can use after six P.M." (The possibilities can include a board game, champagne and two glasses, a television, theater tickets, etc.)
- **His 'n Hers.** Guests are asked to bring gifts that can be enjoyed by the bride as well as the groom, or to bring gifts that come in matching or coordinating pairs. (The possibilities are his-and-hers aprons, towels, robes, coffee mugs, two place settings of tableware, etc.)
- If the shower is just for the bride, some popular themes are **kitchen, lingerie, recipes, linen,** and **personal.**

- A groom-only shower can have such themes as **barware, kitchen, garage and yard, entertaining, hobby,** and **personal.**
- **Happy Holidays.** Guests are encouraged to bring gifts to decorate the couple's home during specific holidays. Presents can run from Christmas tree ornaments to ceramic jack o' lantern candleholders to an Easter basket full of gourmet goodies.
- **Think Pink (or Blue, or Green…).** Whatever happens to be the bride's—or groom's—favorite color can be the theme of the shower. Guests are encouraged to bring something in that color. So that you don't end up with twenty pink bath towels, the hostess might specify in what room of the house the guest's gift might be used, such as "Think pink—for the dining room." This might yield pink table linens, dinner candles, or a pink floral centerpiece. "Think pink—for the bedroom," could bring you bed linens, potpourri, or body lotions.
- **Save-the-Earth.** If the bride and groom are interested in saving the planet's natural resources, guests can honor their values by holding a shower involving Earth-friendly gifts

Graciously accept and acknowledge every gift.

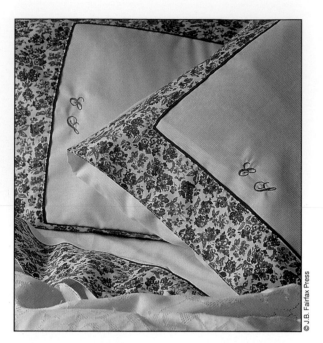

Your new monogram adds a special touch to linens.

such as plants, water-filters, stationery made from recycled paper, cloth (reusable) shopping bags, and donations to an ecologically oriented charity in their name.
- **Family Heritage.** Guests are asked to shower the couple with gifts that reflect their international heritage. These can include products made in the countries of their ancestors, cookbooks offering recipes from those countries, and books on those countries' customs.
- **Collectibles.** If the bride or groom is fond of a certain type of collectible—such as dolls, figurines, plates, thimbles, bells, spoons, and the like—these items can serve as the theme of a shower. For best results, register a preference list with one collectibles store so that you don't end up with duplicates.
- **Initials.** Guests are encouraged to bring gifts that start with the letters in the bride's—or groom's—monogram. For example, if the bride's name is Mary Catherine Smith, then guests are expected to bring gifts that would start with the letters M, C, or S. Examples: M: mixmaster, muslin sheets, Monet (a framed

© William B. Folsom

print of one of the famous artist's masterpieces). C: cookbook, casserole dish, Christmas decorations. S: silverware, sachets, stationery.

The Perfect Shower Gift

While showers are full of guests bringing gifts with the best of intentions, many of the gifts may not be what you can use. Here's where the old cliché "An ounce of prevention is worth a pound of cure" comes into play.

As soon as you know what colors you'll be using in your new home, spread the word. The same can be said for any tableware patterns, cookware, or household furnishings you prefer. Just bring up your preferences in general conversation. Everyone will love to hear the details of your wedding and home preparation. Don't disappoint them or later you'll only disappoint yourself.

If you have registered gift preferences with a local store, talk about the experience to your friends. They'll get the hint and will most likely shop that store—and your list—when it comes to gift-buying time.

Whatever you do, remember that it is in poor taste to ask for cash gifts. If friends know that funds would be appreciated, they might put together a "bouquet of bucks"—a nosegay of flowers intermixed with money—but do not request such gifts.

Chances are that even with all your groundwork laid, someone will still show up with a gift that is totally wrong in color or useless in purpose. Remember, sometimes a gift means more to the giver than the receiver. If there is absolutely no way in the world you can live with the gift, your options include:

- Look at the box in which the gift came and search for the name of the store from which it was purchased. Make an exchange quietly.
- Graciously tell the giver that as much as you appreciate the gift, it just doesn't complement your new home and a replacement would be appreciated. Most likely, the giver

will give you the receipt and ask you to select
something you prefer.

- Put the item away and only take it out for display when the giver visits.

- Donate the item to a church or charity bazaar—
hopefully one in which the gift-giver is not in
attendance.

- Whatever you do, don't rewrap the item and
give it away to someone else—especially someone who attended your shower or might also
know the gift's original giver. You're only asking
for trouble if you let the white elephant inten-
tionally pass into other hands. Besides, once
you give it to someone else, you're saying that
the bright green statue of Venus with the clock
in her stomach reflects your taste!

A Gracious Guest of Honor

As guest of honor, you don't have to worry about
following a theme, but that doesn't let you off the
hook. There are still obligations you have to meet.

- Even if you know of the shower, act surprised.
You owe it to your hostess and her guests.

- Be gracious throughout the event. Don't com-
plain about the way you look or how you can't
understand why anyone would give you such a
useless gift. You're on stage and everyone is
watching. Chances are, someone in the crowd is
also taking notes…which will be read out loud
sometime before the shower is over.

- Even though you thanked everyone in person
for their gifts and participation, written thank-
you notes are also required. These should be
sent within ten days. Each note should say
something personal, not just "Thank you for the
lovely gift." Mention the gift by name and add a
personal touch such as "Thank you for the
lovely waffle iron. John and I will get lots of use
and enjoyment out of it."

- Send a thank-you gift to the host/hostess.
A bouquet of flowers or basket of fruit is
appropriate.

© FPG International

Whether or not it is your first, every wedding is a celebration of life and love. What's past is just that— over. Weddings are a promise to the future.

Second Time Around

Just because you're getting married again doesn't grant you immunity from being honored at showers. Far from it. If it's been a while since your first marriage—and you've changed location, jobs, and even friends since then—be prepared for quite a few rounds of surprise events.

If you fall into this category, chances are you already have more household furnishings and supplies than you need. As such, showers will probably follow along the lines of lingerie, gourmet products, and romantic gifts. Your friends know you've been married before, but so what? Everyone will want to help you celebrate a new beginning, a fresh start. Let them share in your newfound happiness. Never suggest a no-gift shower. Even though you might think you have everything you can ever possibly need for the rest of your life, sharing gifts is part of the fun for you and your guests. Don't begrudge yourself or your friends that good time. Surely they know you are living in a well-furnished home, but allow them to use their imaginations to come up with unique presents that will remind you of them and

you'll probably enjoy more than you thought possible.

At your shower you're the honored guest. Act like one. Let each guest know you are happy she is there. Go with the flow and smile!

The Bachelor and Bachelorette Bash

Because the traditional wedding shower has become coed, bachelor or bucks' parties and bachelorette or hens' parties are taking on new importance… and rituals!

What happens at a men's-only party is entirely private. As the bride you must remember that yes, of course he respects you and of course he'll be careful, but he also isn't the one who planned the party nor does he have control over the situation. If you later find out what went on and aren't too happy about it, don't take it out on him. Give him the benefit of the doubt and live happily ever after.

The same holds true for the bride's night out. As with the groom's bash, everything will be planned all in fun. Both bride and groom should keep in mind that if things get out of hand, they can tactfully bow out of a situation without hurting anyone's feelings.

Whether you're the bride or groom, watch out for cameras. If your party includes activities that might be misconstrued by others, for the sake of your future happiness, prevent all pictures. Some scenes are best left to memory.

If you have a hen or bachelorette party, chances are it will be as casual and informal as possible, but that still doesn't let you off the hook from sending out proper thank-you notes. Your friends went through trouble and expense on your behalf. Send each a note saying what a good and/or unforgettable time you had and how you will always remember their participation in making it all possible.

A Final Note

The final "shower" belongs to you. Within ten days prior to the wedding, plan an appreciation party for all those who helped to make your wedding special. Be sure to include all attendants and anyone else who went out of their way on your behalf. It'll give you the perfect opportunity to give them your thank-you gifts and to tell them how much you appreciate their thoughtfulness.

THE BRIDE AND GROOM
THE MAID OR MATRON
OF HONOR
THE BEST MAN
OTHER ATTENDANTS
PARENTAL PREFERENCES

The Wedding Party
and Their Duties

In its most fantasy-filled sense, a wedding is the joining of two people as one couple. But, in reality, it's the joining of two families and sets of friends as one very large unit.

You may only have eyes for him and he may only have eyes for you, but rest assured there will be plenty of eyes on both of you throughout the wedding. Luckily, many of those eyes will belong to people who are there to help you make it through what is frequently referred to as "the happiest day of your life." If everyone performs their duties well, it might be just that.

Since you will be the one wearing the sweeping white gown that everyone wants to inspect and critique, you'll be the center of attention. There's no way of getting around it—but there are ways to make sure you are at your all-time best.

Your first duty as a bride is to yourself. Be good to yourself. Be sure all arrangements for everything have been completed at least one week in advance: that your gown, shoes, and accessories fit, the florist knows your address, and everything else is just the way it should be.

This is your time to relax and pamper yourself like never before—because you'll never have the opportunity again!

Have your nails done. Get that facial and massage you've always wanted. Catch up on the motion pictures you've wanted to see. At the very least, the seventy-two hours before the wedding should belong to you.

As strange as this may sound, get plenty of rest, too. Think of how many brides you've seen who looked as if they were pulled through the mill before they even finished the wedding ceremonies; all the brides that stifled yawns at their own weddings, trying their best to keep their eyes open and heads up. Why? Because they fussed and fretted up to the last-minute. Don't let that happen to you.

If there's a last-minute problem, let someone else handle it. Your mother, sister, or maid of honor can be called to duty, but not you. The only bags related to your wedding should be those in which you packed your honeymoon clothes—not bags under your eyes.

THE BRIDE AND GROOM

When it comes to the wedding itself, your work is just about over. It's your wedding. Enjoy it! Be at the place of the ceremony on time. It might be fashionable to keep your date waiting, but not your groom— and certainly not a room full of people.

Since you visited the place of the ceremony before, you know the layout. If the location has a dressing room, make a last minute stop to do some final primping. A few minutes later, you'll probably be photographed more often than any other time in your life. As the music starts, hold your father's or escort's arm and walk with dignity. Take slow but sure steps. Every eye in the place will be on you. Savor the moment.

Once you have reached your groom, it's show time! A wedding is much like a play in the theater. You and your groom are the stars, the attendants are the supporting cast, the guests are the audience, and

© Sandra Fisk/The Stock Agency

Relax. Enjoy your last days as a single person while you anticipate the togetherness ahead. This is one of the best times of your life. Enter this new phase without a worry or a care.

Signing the marriage license is the last step to being "officially married." It's a serious event, but can be fun since your maid-of-honor and best man are with you as witnesses.

the person officiating is the director. Like good stars, you should listen to the director and follow every cue. Most likely the director has gone through dozens of ceremonies before yours. Rely on that experience!

Recite your part clearly and loud enough for everyone to hear. All ears will be waiting to hear those famous words. If you flub the words, don't worry about it—keep going. The classic flub was when Princess Diana, then Lady Diana Spencer, mixed up Prince Charles' middle names during the ceremony—and that was in front of television cameras beaming the event to millions of people around the world. Without any fuss, she continued her speech and won the hearts and admiration of everyone along with it.

Immediately after the ceremony, chances are you'll be required to stand in a receiving line to acknowledge guests. Be sure your shoes are comfortable—you've got a lot of standing to do. Greet each guest sincerely but quickly. Of course you won't remember everyone's name, nor will you have a chance to make small talk. That can come later. Just smile, be polite, thank everyone for their compliments, and continue until the last guest is eagerly waiting outside for your grand exit…before which a few duties will probably have to be met, such as signing the marriage license.

Most likely your photographer will suggest taking formal photos at the site of the ceremony. It's a very appropriate location, but don't let the shutter snap until you've had time to revisit the powder room. After all, you've just stood in line for about half an hour greeting guests, getting touched, kissed, hugged, and admired. Your makeup will probably be in need of repair and your outfit will need some fluffing. The few minutes you take for redoing them will save you years of regret later. (Share that tip with your groom. After all, it's his wedding, too.)

Once at the reception location, remember, you're still on display. You don't have to be rigid, but you certainly don't want to let yourself go either. Another receiving line will be waiting for you. Here you can take more time chatting with each guest, but still limit the conversation. Rely on the wedding director to give you guidance. If no director exists, use your best judgment.

Eat! Too many former brides will tell you that they never had a chance to eat at their weddings. As such, they felt faint during the reception and had hunger headaches afterward—not the best way to start a honeymoon! Take your time and enjoy the meal you selected. Everyone can wait to see your gown and extend their best wishes.

Your maid of honor is your second-closest companion throughout the wedding. Rely on her to help you with your flowers, gown, going-away outfit, and any other tasks that require a helping hand. She is there to see that your requests are fulfilled; she will participate with dignity and delight.

© Ron Chapple/FPG International

Be sure to send word to the bandleader that you don't want any dance music until after you've completed your meal. Otherwise, just as you pick up your fork, some well-meaning uncle will drag you out on the dance floor. He'll be followed by what will seem like every other man in the room, and by the time you get back to the table, your dinner will be cold or back in the kitchen. If there is no dance music, there will be no dancing—until you are ready.

Back to the wedding director. Yes, he or she is more experienced at conducting a wedding, but it's *your wedding.* You don't have to go along with every suggestion, plus you can make a few of your own. And just because "everyone does it," doesn't mean you have to. For example, if you think the custom of throwing the bride's garter is in poor taste, then don't do it. Nor do you and your groom have to feed each other cake—let alone squash cake in each other's faces!

After the reception, it's off to the honeymoon and your new life. All that's left for you to do in terms of the wedding is to send out thank-you notes, select your final pictures, and reminisce.

Of course, it's his wedding, too, but alas, as handsome as the groom may be, the bride gets top hon-ors. Don't worry about his ego; it'll hold up just fine. If you incorporated some of his ideas into the overall scheme of the wedding, he should have no problems at all.

The groom's day should start very much like yours. He should be well rested and ready for a lot of special activities ahead. Being properly suited and at the place of the ceremony on time are his first duties of the day. His duties throughout the ceremony, receiving line, and photography session are the same as yours.

At the reception, he should be your protector from sincere but pushy well-wishers and your escort

Bridal gown designed by Michele Piccione for Alfred Angelo

throughout the evening. Advise him in advance of any and all changes you may want and didn't discuss beforehand.

Before the wedding, the two of you should have worked out a time plan, so that you are in accord as to when to leave the reception. After the wedding, he too can pitch in with writing thank-you notes and selecting photos.

THE MAID OR MATRON OF HONOR

The maid, or matron of honor, if she lives up to her title, should be your lady-in-waiting throughout the wedding day—from almost the minute you awaken to the moment you leave for your honeymoon.

Rely on her to hold the groom's wedding ring, help you with your gown, hold your bouquet during the ceremony, be sure that your gown is picture-perfect throughout the day, make certain all the attendants are where they should be, and be your best friend.

Other functions she should be able to handle are:

• Be in attendance at all prenuptial events
• Help you address invitations and place cards
• Help you pack for your honeymoon
• Be sure bridesmaids—including the flower girl —are at all the fittings, rehearsal, and ceremony on time
• Witness and sign the marriage certificate after the ceremony
• Participate in the receiving line by standing to the groom's left
• Help you dress for your honeymoon
• Take care of your gown after the reception, bringing it to the cleaners, your home, or wherever you wish

While you may want your best friend to be your maid of honor, if you are to have a religious cere-mony, check with the clergy member first. Some religions have strict rules about who can be the offi-cial witness. It may have to be a member of that reli-gion or someone who has attended pre-ceremony instruction classes.

THE BEST MAN

What your maid of honor is to you, the best man is to your groom. He's the guy's backup support and should be able to handle everything from getting the groom dressed and to church on time to making sure all the groom's wedding-related expenses are paid and providing you (if necessary) with transportation to the honeymoon site, airport, or wherever.

Other duties that can be assigned to the best man are:

- Help the groom pack for the honeymoon
- Make sure the groom has the marriage license with him
- Give payment to clergy or ceremony officiant
- Hold bride's ring until it is needed for the ceremony
- Be sure all ushers—and ring bearer—are properly attired and well behaved throughout the wedding
- Be the first at the reception in order to welcome the bride and groom
- Serve as toastmaster at the bride's table at the reception and give the first toast to the bride and groom at the ceremony as well as at the rehearsal dinner
- Help in welcoming guests and making introductions
- Dance with the bride, maid of honor, both mothers, and single female guests
- Sign wedding certificate after the ceremony
- Help groom get ready for the honeymoon
- Take care of groom's wedding outfit after the reception, returning it to the rental shop, cleaners, home, or wherever the groom wishes

OTHER ATTENDANTS

The easiest tasks of all belong to the bridesmaids. They've helped with the shower, maybe assisted the bride in packing and arranging things for the new home, but basically they're there for moral support and to help dress up the look of the wedding.

They're there because they are close friends and relatives of the bride and were wanted to share the special day in a special way.

Specific duties they should gladly perform include:

- Attend all prenuptial special events, fittings, etc.
- Give you lots of moral support throughout the day—and prenuptial moments of anxiety
- Dance with single men at the reception
- Assist you in any way possible

The ushers, on the other hand, are "on duty" throughout the wedding. Before the ceremony, they should decorate any cars and make sure everyone is in their proper seats before the bride comes down the aisle. Be sure to coach the ushers during rehearsal about proper seating arrangements: The bride's mother gets seated last; the groom's mother before that; and any grandmothers before that; and any special guests before that.

The ushers should also act as "crowd controllers" when guests exit the place of the ceremony and enter the reception site. Also rely on them to do any errands or handle any problems that might occur throughout the day. By all means, be sure the groom names a head usher. There are plenty of responsibilities that only he can fulfill—especially if the best man is preoccupied with his own chores.

The head usher should be called upon to:

- Be sure all female guests have the proper corsages or flowers and are treated in the proper manner
- Escort your mother and the groom's mother down the aisle and into their proper places at the ceremony
- Seat special guests according to your instructions
- Make sure the wedding party is at the proper place and in order for photographs
- Make sure all the duties performed by the ushers are done so properly
- Check that boutonnieres are proper and are worn on the left side, stem down
- Make sure that any flowers that are to be removed from the ceremony to the reception site or other location are done so properly
- Make sure that the guests adhere to the synagogue or church's laws regarding the throwing of rice, confetti, etc. after the ceremony

(This last item may sound strange, but due to the growing concern about ecological matters, many towns have regulations forbidding the throwing of rice and confetti and the use of balloons. Check with the town clerk and person who is to officiate at the ceremony before you or your guests end up in an embarrassing situation.)

Children can be a delightful or a detrimental part of the wedding. The general rule of thumb is not to have any children under the age of five or older than eight in the party. Younger than five could be too difficult to handle, older than eight could be indifferent to the entire wedding.

You know the children best, but also use your best judgment. Little Sally might be cute playing at home, but how will she react when she's being stared at by a crowd of strangers in a strange location? Also, do you want to compete for attention with a precocious and adorable six-year old?

© J.B. Fairfax Press

© Cindi Kinney/The Stock Agency

If you should decide to have children in the wedding party, give strict instructions to their parents, your bridesmaids, the ushers, and the children themselves as to what they are to do and what's expected of them.

Parental Preferences

While it may be your wedding, it is not your party. Remind yourself of whose names are on the invitation: your parents! It is they who are inviting others to the wedding. As such, they are the host and hostess. Don't expect to see too much of them, but on the other hand be sure they receive the respect and special attention they so rightly deserve.

Your mother should be the last person seated at the ceremony—right before the first bridesmaid starts down the aisle. If anyone comes in after her, that person should find their own seat—by using the side aisle.

Your mother should be part of the receiving line after the ceremony, should be consulted throughout all pre-wedding preparations if she is paying for them, and generally sets the tone of the wedding.

Two questions often come up concerning the mothers of the bride and groom: Who gets to pick the color the mothers should wear? Is it possible to give the mother of the bride something special to do during the ceremony?

The answer to the first question is the bride's mother. As hostess of the wedding, she selects the color she wishes to wear before the groom's mother. She should then tell the groom's mother of her choice of color—so that the dresses do not clash in style and color and also so that they are not *too* similar.

As to the second question, there are many ways the bride's mother can be more than just a spectator at the wedding. Some brides ask their mothers to help escort them down the aisle. However, this can be awkward and distracting. It is better for the mother to do a special reading during the ceremony, or when the officiant asks, "Who gives this woman in marriage?," both parents can answer, "We do." Ask the officiant for other suggestions.

The father of the bride has always had a special place at the wedding. In addition to escorting the bride down the aisle and sharing in her moment of glory, he answers the question of who gives the bride away, greets guests in the receiving line, and gets the second dance with the bride. Tradition gives him special treatment because he is, after all, the official host of the wedding.

It's customary for him to be dressed in a similar fashion to the ushers in the wedding party, but that's not the strictest of rules. After all, he's still his wife's escort. Whatever he feels is most presentable is most proper.

Duties the bride's parents should take care of together are:

- Make all guests feel welcome, especially those on the groom's side and from out of town
- Invite the groom's parents to dinner soon after the engagement to get acquainted with them and discuss any wedding suggestions or special requirements they may have
- Make hotel and restaurant suggestions to out-of-town guests
- Assist the bride in wedding plans
- Pay for bride's wedding clothing, personal trousseau, linen trousseau
- Pay for invitations, announcements, attendants' and ceremony flowers
- Pay for bridal portraits and all wedding photography
- Pay for reception, decorations, and wedding cake
- Pay for ceremony location expenses, including music and decorations
- Provide transportation for the wedding party to and from the ceremony
- Select and present bride and her new husband with a wedding gift

Just as your parents will be the official host and hostess of the wedding, the groom's parents are very special guests. It is only polite to consult with them about your wedding plans. His parents should discuss these with your parents and be ready to pay, if your parents feel necessary, for any specifications that are required. These can include special meals to meet a groom's relative's dietary restrictions or to inviting more personal guests than your parents may be able to afford.

As stated previously, the groom's mother should follow your mother's wishes on what should and should not be worn at the wedding. She should also be the liaison between your family and friends and the groom's.

Should anyone on the groom's side of the family wish to give you a shower, his mother should see to it that your mother and maid of honor are invited.

Other obligations the groom's parents should be ready to fulfill include:

- Participating in the receiving line
- Pay for the bride's flowers if the groom cannot meet that obligation
- Provide the bride's parents with a personal guest list within the limits set by her parents
- Present the bride and groom with an appropiate wedding gift
- Host the rehearsal dinner, if any
- Notify the head usher of any special guests from their side that might be attending the wedding so that proper arrangements can be made

Grandparents, favorite relatives, childhood friends, and others may be special guests at your wedding. They deserve special attention, but not at the sake of the other guests.

If there are people with whom you are especially close who are not part of the wedding party and with whom you want to spend private moments, your wedding is not the place for such meetings. Plan on spending time with those people the day before the wedding, but not at the wedding itself. You simply won't have the opportunity.

If possible, assign such people to perform special duties to make them active participants in the wedding. If your reception is going to include a tea, ask special female guests to do the honor of pouring. Special guests might also perform readings at your wedding. If any have exceptional musical talent, ask them to sing or play at your wedding. You can also make arrangements for special guests to sit in key locations at the ceremony and reception.

THE BRIDAL GOWN
ECONOMICS
THE GROOM'S ATTIRE

Wedding Clothes

*I*n *today's overall wedding picture, anything and* everything that the couple wishes to wear is acceptable wedding attire. Of course, the traditional frothy white wedding gown and the black tuxedo still rank as the most popular choices, but they aren't the only options. If your wedding has a theme, such as "Fairy Tales Come True," you might want to dress up as Cinderella and the groom as Prince Charming. Should Victorian or Edwardian be a period you mutually admire, there's no reason why you both couldn't or shouldn't dress up in appropiate cloth-

ing. Perhaps either of your ethnic heritages involves costumes or dress customs you have always found wonderful. If so, incorporate them in your wedding attire. Should you stray from the norm, be sure your attendants and key guests (such as parents) follow along. While, yes, it is your wedding, you don't want to look like sore thumbs. Your choice of clothing sets the tone and mood for the entire wedding. The apparel worn by your attendants and the decorations at your wedding should complement your choice of theme.

If you decide to wear pure white, you have plenty of company. Statistics show that 73 percent of all brides will make the same decision. Ivory is a distant second choice at 17 percent; white or ivory with color accents ranks third with 5 percent; white/ivory combination is fourth with 2 percent; pastel colors take fifth place with 2 percent; and all other color choices make up the remaining one percent. No longer a symbol of virginity, white is a color of joy, freshness, and new beginnings. Let your sparkling white wedding gown usher you into a new life.

The style of your dress is a different matter. Of course you'll want something that best flatters your figure, but here's where decorum standards should come into play. The time and mood of your wedding should be kept in mind when selecting the "right" dress. Speaking from a customary point of view, the chart to the right will help you.

THE BRIDAL GOWN

Unless you someday expect to take an oath of office as the head of a government, chances are your wedding dress will be the most important attire of your life—or at least the one in which you will be photographed most. It is not a purchase you make due to price or current fashions. It is the purchase you make according to what looks best on you and feels the most comfortable. Even if you buy your dress off the rack at a department store or specialized wedding dress shop, it is still your dress, and it should suit your features and figure so you look especially lovely in it.

Dressmakers and fashion consultants will ask you a battery of questions about what you like or don't like. They'll also use a terminology that, unless you are the most experienced seamstress, you'll find odd and confusing. If you don't understand any of the jargon used, ask for a definition in layman's terms. After all, you don't want to agree to an "antebellum waist" if you really have no idea what it is and really want a Basque waistline.

		BRIDE	BRIDESMAIDS	MOTHERS	GROOM & USHERS
VERY FORMAL	**EVENING**	Dress: White, ivory, or pastel tints. Long train and elaborate fabrics. Headdress: Veil, long or full. Accessories: Long gloves with short-sleeve dress; shoes to match. Bouquet or flower-trimmed prayer book; simple jewelry; pale hosiery.	Dress: Floor-length, short or long sleeves, in colors to complement wedding colors. Train optional. Headdress: Cap or hat. Short veil optional. Accessories: Gloves in white or pale tints to complement sleeve lengths. Floral bouquets. Shoes to match or complement.	Dress: Floor-length evening or dinner dress in compatible color. Hat: Small hat or veil matching or contrasting with dress. Accessories: Gloves (optional) and corsage to complement small handbag.	Clothes: Black tailcoat with matching trousers. White waistcoat, stiff front shirt with wing collar. Accessories: White bow tie, black patent pumps or oxfords. Black socks; white gloves and black silk hat (optional).
	DAY	Same as very formal evening. Fabrics may be less elaborate and a short train is also appropriate.	Dress: Same as Very Formal (Evening), but fabric and styles are usually less elaborate.	Dress: Floor-length, not as formal or elaborate as for evening. Hat and Accessories: Same as Evening.	Clothes: Cutaway coat, gray striped trousers, gray waistcoat, formal white dress shirt with wing collar. Accessories: Tie (ascot or four-in-hand), striped black socks, gray gloves, black silk hat (optional).
SEMI-FORMAL	**EVENING**	Dress: Long white, ivory, or pastel tints, with a chapel or sweep train. Headdress: Fingertip length. Accessories: Same as in Very Formal Weddings.	Dress: Long but occasionally shorter lengths, similar to Very Formal. Headdress and Accessories: Same as Very Formal.	Dress: Long. Hat and Accessories: Same as in Semi-formal (Day).	Clothes: Winter: Black dinner jacket and trousers; vest, white dress shirt with turned-down collar. Summer: White dinner jacket with black trouser, cummerbund; white dress shirt. Accessories: Black shoes, black socks, bow tie, gray gloves.
	DAY	Same as Formal (Evening) but less elaborate fabrics. An elaborate short dress with a bridal headdress is also acceptable.	Dress: May be long or street-length, but not as elaborate as evening. Headdress and Accessories: Same as Evening.	Dress: Street-length dresses or suits. Hat and Accessories: To match and harmonize.	Clothes: Oxford gray stroller with gray striped trousers, gray waistcoat, white shirt with turned-down collar. Accessories: Striped four-in-hand, black shoes, black socks, gray gloves, black homburg (optional).
INFORMAL	**EVENING**	Dress: Floor-length of white and tints in trainless style. Headdress: Veil, short to elbow length. Accessories: Same as for Formal with a simpler bouquet.	Dress: Street-length permissible if bride wears floor-length, or same length as bride. Headdress: Hat or small headpiece with or without short veil to match the bride's. Accessories: Small bouquet, other accessories compatible with dress and wedding party.	Dress: Street-length dresses with appropriate accessories and hat.	Clothes: Dark gray or navy business suit, white shirt. Summer: Also acceptable—white linen jacket with oxford gray trousers; white suit; dark blue jacket with white or gray flannel trousers. Accessories: Subdued tie and hose, black shoes.
	DAY	Dress: Street-length in white or pastels. Headdress: Short, very full veil. Accessories: Small bouquet or flower-covered prayer book.	Same as Informal (Evening) but with a simpler style and fabric.	Same as Informal (Evening), but not as elaborate.	Same as Informal (Evening).
VERY INFORMAL	**DAY & EVENING**	Dress: Suit or street dress. Headdress: Bridal hat or short veil. Accessories: Corsage or nosegay; suitable white gloves and shoes.	Dress: Suit or outfit similar in style to that of the bride. Headdress: Hat. Accessories: Corsage.	Street-length dress or suit similar to attendants with head covering and corsage.	Same as Informal (Evening).

Wedding Gown Glossary

Here's a brief glossary of some terms you might encounter while selecting a wedding dress. And, again, if terms are used that you don't understand—ask! It's your wedding and you will end up wearing the final results of the style conversation. Be sure you understand everything that's being said, and don't be talked into purchasing anything that isn't exactly right for you.

A-line—skirt design has a flared hem and a close-fitting waist. The waist to the hem of the skirt resemble the letter "A"

Ankle length—the skirt is slightly off the floor. It reaches your ankles

Antebellum waist—natural waistline that dips about two inches to a point in the center front

Appliqué—decoration sewn onto the dress

Apron—an overskirt joined at the back of the waist

Ballerina skirt—a full skirt of filmy or net material that reveals the ankles

Basque waistline—also called "dropped," it falls about two inches below the natural waistline

Bateau neckline—a boat-shaped neckline that forms a straight line between the shoulders

Bell sleeve—full-length sleeve that flares slightly from the shoulder to the wrist

Blusher—short veil that covers your face

Bouffant—very full skirt or veil

Brush train—short train that just "brushes" the floor as you walk

Bugle beads—short tubular beads used for decoration

Bustle—large gathering of fabric used as a decorative detail at the back of the dress

Cameo neckline—high neckline of sheer fabric decorated with a lace circle of brooch material at center front

Cap sleeve—short, fitted sleeve that barely covers the top of the arm

Cathedral train—a piece of fabric that extends three yards from the waist

Chapel train—a piece of fabric that extends about five feet from the waist

Contoured waistline—very close fitting at the natural waistline

Court train—a piece of train that extends about three feet from the waist

Decolletage—a plunging neckline that reveals breast cleavage

Detachable train—the train of the gown is attached by hooks or snaps, and can be quickly undone to remove the train for dancing

Dolman sleeve—sleeve is very wide at armhole and tight at wrist, usually cut in one piece with bodice

Dropped waistline—see "Basque waistline"

Empire waistline—waistline is created by skirt being attached to the bodice just below the bustline

Fitted bodice—fabric hugs the upper part of the body

Floor length—the hem falls one half to a full inch from the floor and is no longer than the tip of the shoes

Full sleeve—set at shoulder and runs to wrist with no fitting

Headband—fabric strip that circles the head, wrapping around the center of the forehead

Gauntlet—arm covering with no fingers worn in place of traditional gloves

Juliet cap—close-fitting headpiece that covers crown

Leg of mutton sleeve—very puffy at shoulder with a fitted forearm

Long-fitted sleeve—set at shoulder and runs to wrist with no fullness

Natural waistline—bodice and skirt join at your own waistline

Picture hat—very large-brimmed hat, often decorated with flowers and ribbons

Portrait neckline—fabric is crisscrossed over the bodice to give special attention to the shoulders

Puff sleeve—short, full sleeve that runs from the shoulder to just above the elbow

Queen Anne neckline—high on the sides and back with an angled open bodice with a sweetheart shape

Raised waistline—waist of dress is gathered one to two inches above your natural waistline to allow more fullness in the skirt

Royal train—longest of all trains, extends more than nine feet from the waist

Sheath—straight, semi-fitted gown with no definite waistline

Short sleeve—set at shoulder and runs with very little fullness to the middle of the upper arm

Sweep train—fabric extends six inches on the floor

Fabric Glossary

Batiste—sheer with a plain or figured weave

Brocade—woven with an elaborate, raised-pattern edge

Chantilly Lace—made of silk or linen with a six-sided mesh ground and a scrolled or floral design

Charmuse—pliable satin fabric of silk or manmade materials

Crepe—thin, soft, lightweight fabric highlighted by a crinkled surface

Crepe de Chine—crepe but with a softer feel

Faille—shiny material of silk, cotton, or polyester with a closely woven design that causes slight ribs in the welt

Georgette—sheer crepe highlighted by a dull texture

Illusion—very thin transparent silk tulle used for veils

Moire—silk or polyester highlighted with a "rings of circles" design; frequently called "watered silk"

Organza—sheer with a plain weave

Organdy—transparent, usually of muslin, with a stiff finish

Peau de soie—silk woven to have a shiny finish

Plisse—crepe that has been treated to have permanent crinkles

Satin—silk or polyester with a smooth, shiny surface

Taffeta—plain woven fabric with a crisp finish

Tulle—sheer, stiff silk or synthetic fabric often used for veils

It's only natural for all eyes to be on the bride. The selection of wedding gowns is endless and yours should be as flattering as possible. Rely on the perfect fit and style to make you look nothing short of beautiful from all angles.

ECONOMICS

The cost of wedding dresses will vary according to the fabric and ornamentation. Style tends not to be a costly matter. In 1990, the average wedding dress costs $800 though some cost much more.

The time you spend selecting the right dress should be matched with that for selecting the right headpiece. Don't settle for anything less than exactly what you want and what looks best on you. A word of advice: When trying on headpieces, your hair should be identical to how it will be at the wedding. Many a headpiece didn't look or feel right at the wedding due to a change in hairstyle.

The selection of headpieces to choose from is endless, running from full crowns of rhinestones to a simple flower behind the ear. The style of your dress will dictate the best choice. The most popular headpieces are: floral wreath, crown/tiara, floral comb, veil, Juliet cap, headband, picture hat. In the early 1990s, the average amount spent on a headpiece was $170.

Popular Preference

The most popular lengths are (in order): floor length with chapel train; floor length with cathedral train; floor length with court train; floor length with sweep train; floor length with longer than cathedral train.

The most popular necklines are: sweetheart, high lace, off shoulder, plunging, boat.

The most popular waistlines are: basque, natural, dropped, contoured, raised.

The most popular sleeve lengths are: long-fitted, puff, full, short, sleeveless.

The most popular fabrics are: satin, taffeta, silk, lace, organza.

© Sandra Fisk/The Stock Agency

Give yourself plenty of time to shop for the right outfit, and allow your seamstress plenty of time to make it picture-perfect. Six months is a minimum. If possible, give yourself ten months.

Attendants Attention

Thousands of years ago, attendants wore the same outfit as the bride in order to confuse evil spirits who might be jealous of her happiness and harm her. Today all that has changed. Your attendants should not look like "other brides," but should instead wear outfits that complement yours. The most popular selection of bride's attendant's dresses are tea-length or floor-length and in a pastel or other solid color. Can attendants wear white? If you so desire, but remember, by doing so, they'll detract attention from you. Can attendants wear black? Again, the

choice is yours. If you want your attendants in black, it's best to have them carry brightly colored flowers.

There is no rule that demands every attendant wear the same dress. As such, you don't have to make your attendants victims of tradition if that is not in their best interest. If your attendants happen to be a range of sizes, chances are each woman would probably look best in a different style. All dresses, however, should be the same length and can be the same color.

Your mother can choose whatever style or color of dress she prefers. However, as hostess, she sets the tone for all other female guests. The most popular choices are tea-length or street-length in a pastel or other solid color. Can your mother wear white or black? Of course, but why would she want to? You should be the center of attention.

Your attendants will be there to give you moral support as well as to "dress up" your wedding. Share your feelings and ideas with them. They've been important to you in your life; make them an important part of this special day, too.

Accessories

Finish your perfect outfit with the perfect accessories. Here is a checklist of the most popular:

- **Decorated shoes**
- **Hosiery**
- **Earrings**
- **Garter**
- **Lingerie**
- **Neck jewelry (pearls, chains, et cetera)**
- **Handkerchief**
- **Gloves**

Your wedding ring and engagement ring should be all you need on your hands. You'll not want anything else since your left hand will be the center of attention. Because of that—and the fact that it will be your special day—be good to yourself and your body. Treat yourself to the most wonderful beauty products and services you can find. In addition to a hairdresser, get a professional manicure, makeup application, facial, and pedicure.

The Groom's Attire

The old song may go, "Here comes the bride," but it's his wedding, too. No matter what the time or tone of the wedding, there's a formal outfit just right for him. Even with the rainbow of colors waiting at the nearest formal-wear store, his chances of selecting all black are 46 percent. The second most popular choice is gray (16 percent), a white dinner jacket with black pants (15 percent), and all white (9 percent), with any color or combination the store still has to offer remaining.

If he insists on wearing a basic black-tie tuxedo, don't fret over his lack of creativity. He's following 40 percent of all grooms. The second most popular choice is white tie and black tails. Cutaways and strollers fall third and fourth in popularity.

Whatever his outfit might lack in originality can be made up with accessories. The list is an ongoing one that includes a wide selection of jewelry and finishing touches in a plethora of colors. There are shirts with many choices of collars, cummerbunds, vests, ties, ascots, handkerchiefs, hats, and more. If he decides on the pleated shirt with winged collar and black cummerbund, let him enjoy it. That's the most popular choice.

He will spend hours renting or buying the "right" outfit, then add a pair of shoes that are anything but proper. For this reason, you should take a special interest in his footwear. Most likely the store where he rented the suit can also rent him the shoes. If not, be sure he is well (and properly) heeled.

The groom should allow plenty of time for alterations and for the other men in the wedding party to be fitted for coordinating outfits. Six weeks is the minimum.

Whatever outfit the groom selects, he should feel comfortable. The coat should allow free movement of the arms and lie smoothly across the back. The coat should reach to the curl of his fingers when his arms are straight at his sides. The sleeves should reveal a half an inch of shirt cuff. The trousers should be hemmed even with the top of the heel of the shoes in back and offer a slight break in the front, resting on the shoes.

Experience has proven that the groom should try on his complete outfit at least three days prior to the wedding. This allows for any last-minute alterations —and to make sure everything is there. Many a groom has walked down the aisle without the proper studs or shirt, only because he didn't try on the complete outfit or check the accessories beforehand.

Best Man and Ushers

The best man and ushers wear outfits that coordinate with—not match—the groom's. They might wear a different color cummerbund or accesories. The bride's father should wear an outfit similar to that of the best man. It is also proper for the groom's father to wear a matching or coordinating outfit.

As with the groom, the male attendants should try on their complete outfits at least three days before the wedding to ensure everything fits properly and is in place.

Second Wedding Wardrobe

Second wedding? There's no reason why you should have to look second class. You're celebrating a new start. Enjoy it! There's no reason—other than your own preference—why you shouldn't or can't wear a full white, traditional wedding gown. Wear whatever you want and whatever makes you feel most comfortable.

If you went the full white wedding dress route the first time and don't wish to make a repeat performance, opt for a pastel-colored, tea-length dress or a suit. If you want to wear a white gown again, be sure it is a different style than the one you wore to your first wedding. You might also want to wear a subdued headpiece. A few flowers or a picture hat with no veil is a popular choice for the remarrying woman.

Should it be the groom's second wedding, it makes no difference. The bride sets the dress code of the wedding. His black tuxedo can be put to service again without any second thoughts.

Civil Ceremonies

Depending on where you live or your religion, you might have to go through a civil ceremony the day before the full-scale wedding event. This too should be handled as an important part of the wedding picture—because it is. Select a suit or dress and jacket ensemble in a pastel or other solid color for the occasion. A corsage is appropriate. This outfit can later serve as your "going away" attire, worn as you whisk away to your honeymoon.

His clothing for the civil ceremony or visit to the registry office should be a dark-colored suit with white or pastel-colored shirt and four-in-hand tie. Again, these clothes can be used as his "going away" honeymoon attire. (Save the jeans and T-shirts for the honeymoon itself.)

The Trousseau

Officially speaking, the groom's wedding clothing traditions stop the minute the two of you leave for the honeymoon. Yours doesn't; you have a "trousseau." What does a trousseau consist of? It is composed of everything you intend to wear on your honeymoon. What you choose specifically depends on your lifestyle and honeymoon trip. The most popular trousseau items are: sleepwear (including negligees), underwear, sportswear, shoes, dresses and suits, panty hose, evening wear, accessories (belts, scarves, et cetera), sunglasses, robes and loungewear, jewelry, handbags, slips, jeans, tennis and other athletic apparel, and a coat or raincoat. The average amount of money a contemporary bride-to-be spends on her trousseau is $550 though what you spend is up to you and your parents (if they are paying) or your groom (if he is). Also, you will receive many trousseau items as shower gifts.

© FPG International

Once a symbol of fertility, flowers now add softness and beauty to a wedding. Bouquets should be in styles and colors that complement the gowns. Every flower and color has a special meaning, so use them to add personal touches, too. Arrangements can include your favorite flower, flowers of the months of your and the groom's birthdays, or flowers that "speak" of your feelings.

THE BRIDAL REGISTRY
WEDDING GIFT
ETIQUETTE

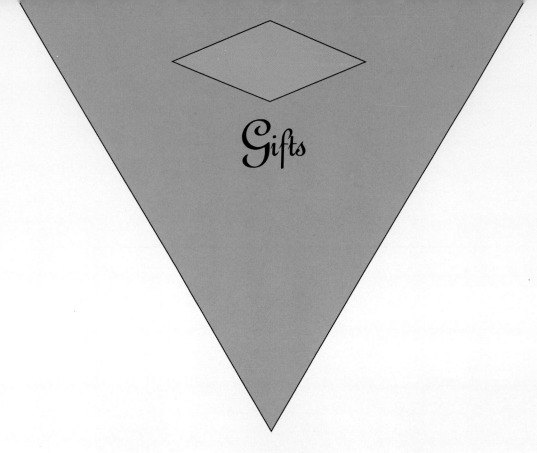

Gifts

*I*s it proper to expect wedding gifts? No. But will you get wedding gifts? Of course! For centuries, this has been a delicate situation. At one time, guests didn't bring wedding gifts since the bride's dowry took care of such matters. Instead, they brought food for the wedding feast. As times changed, the guests laded the couple with wedding gifts instead. Since that time, the big question has been: What do you request—or give, if you are a guest—as a wedding present?

One way for guests to answer this question is to ask the bride's mother or whoever is hosting the wedding of the couple's needs and/or wants. Another is for the bride to rely on the tastes of her wedding guests and hope that they bring gifts that can be used. A third—and much more civilized—idea is for the couple to make out a "wish list." It is simply a piece of paper on which they write down everything they wish to receive as gifts. Be generous, but be realistic.

List the items you'd like for your home, from linens to furnishings. List personal accessories, too, from

Gifts are an important part of every wedding. They allow your guests to "participate" in the start of your new life. Make the giving and receiving process as smooth as possible. Register a "wish list" at your favorite store; it's practical and pleasurable for everyone involved.

© Tony DeMasi

lingerie to skin lotions. List things you like but could never justify for yourself, such as fresh flowers delivered to your door once a month for a year. List your favorite cordials and other spirits. List things you need for both your hobbies (is there a special line of figurines you collect?). List everything and anything you think your guests can afford, but never list money. As much as you may need it, it is still in poor taste to ask for money. It would be the same as asking for donations to pay for the wedding, since you cannot afford to treat your guests properly. If you really do need cash, ask your mother or wedding's hostess to make the suggestion in a gentle way by saying, "Sally and John have everything they need right now, but are saving for a (new house, television, car, vacation or whatever)." Guests will pick up the hint and act accordingly.

THE BRIDAL REGISTRY

When your list is complete, take it to a store or stores that carry the items you would like to receive. This process is called "registering." The store's service representative or wedding consultant will have you complete a form listing everything you wish to receive. That person will then walk you through the store and make suggestions about what other products are available in every department. While it is true that you can register for everything you want, be realistic in your selection. If you know you're guests are more prone to spend $50 instead of $5,000, then there's no use listing the sterling-silver tea set, because you'll never get it.

It costs nothing to register your "wish list," nor does it cost your guest any money to use it. This is a free service. Its purpose is to get your guests to shop at that particular store. It's important that the store keep good records so that you receive gifts you want, not duplicates, and have the easiest gift-giving process possible.

Depending on the store, a registry can be just that —a place where guests can buy from the wish list of gifts you want. Or, the store can be your sanctuary of sanity. Many stores have registrars who are also wedding consultants, and they can answer your prenuptial questions at no cost. Stores often have "holding rooms" in which your gifts can be held until immediately before or after the wedding and delivered together to the location of your choice. Some stores have complimentary display service and will send a decorator to your home or apartment to tastefully display a selection of your wedding gifts for all guests to see and enjoy. Some stores have "package deals" with other retailers and can get you discounts from those suppliers—such as bakers, caterers, and florists—simply because you registered there. Some stores also have ongoing registry services, which means that after the wedding, the consultant will continue to work with you in acquiring everything you wished for. She will notify you of sales, take care of exchanges of unwanted gifts and help in other related matters.

With today's wedding market being so lucrative, it is difficult to find a store that doesn't offer some kind of registry service. Shop around for the registry that offers the best services. Register at more than one store, too—especially if the groom is from another city. His friends might be more comfortable shopping at a local store. Give them that option.

Another option is to register at one local store that has multiple branches, with one in the hometown of the groom or long-distance relatives. Most major department stores have shop-by-phone service, so there's no reason why anyone—no matter where they live—can't take advantage of your wish list.

If the store with which you are registering gives you a gift just for doing so, don't be surprised—it's customary. It's glad to have your business. Other perks a store might use to make you and your guests happy is to give you a gift certificate for up to 10 percent of the business your wedding generated. This is normally presented thirty days after the wedding—when all returns have been made. It is also common for the store to give you a placesetting of your chosen dinnerware pattern if your guests have purchased all but one from your list. Stores want and need your business. Let them be generous to you. You've been kind to them.

Just because you have selected a store to hold your wish list doesn't give you the right to be abusive. The consultant is just that—a consultant. He or she is not your best friend, psychiatrist, substitute mother, or referee. Consultants are professionals and should be treated as such.

You have no right to expect anything more from that store than you do from any other retail establishment. Holding your registry list doesn't mean the store has to allow you to take back a gift you don't want if it wasn't purchased from that store, nor does it mean it will bend its return policies and give you cash in return for your gifts. It's a business.

Watch out for the "guaranteed sale." This is a marketing concept being practiced by more and more stores. Under this policy, the store makes an imprint of your major credit card and bills you for everything on your registry list that is not purchased by your guests. Essentially, the store makes you guarantee that you will buy everything the others haven't. This could be very costly to you. If the store has such a policy, beware and be wise. Some stores might require a "guaranteed sale" for special purchases—that is, items you want that they don't usually carry in inventory. If such is the case, it's up to you to proceed or move on.

The most popular wedding gifts are traditional tableware, such as china, crystal, and silverware. Serving pieces in each of those categories come next, but don't limit your wish list to the usual merchandise. Show your creativity and individualism. Wish for gifts that are right for you.

WEDDING GIFT ETIQUETTE

No matter how hard you try to encourage guests to buy from your wish list, there will always be a percentage of people who will give you whatever they want—even if it doesn't fit your decorating scheme. What can you do? One option is to use it anyway, but the more common move is to return it for something else. This can be a delicate situation. Gently tell the giver how much you really love the item, but since it doesn't fit in with your lifestyle, you'd prefer to exchange it for something more suitable. If you do it in a nice way, the giver shouldn't have a problem —unless, of course, the item was handcrafted by the giver! In this case, bite your tongue and find a place for it in the back of a closet.

The only time returning gifts becomes a major matter is if the wedding never takes place. No matter what the reason, if the wedding is cancelled, all gifts must go back—to the givers, not the stores. Even though the givers give with best intentions, if there is no wedding, you have no right to the gifts. If any of the gifts have already been used or spent, you are expected to make proper reimbursement to the givers.

Displaying gifts is a tradition of bygone days that is discussed occasionally. Where gift displays were once done to impress guests by showing the couple's larder, today it's generally considered in poor taste, a public show of guests' tastes and level of generosity. What was once considered a major part of sharing the wedding's joy is now considered shopping competition. This custom also fell out of favor when weddings for the most part were held only infrequently in the home of the bride's parents. When

wedding receptions moved to banquet halls, hotels, and other locations, security suddenly became a problem and having unwrapped gifts on full display became a risk. If you want to show special guests all your gifts, do so privately before or after the wedding.

Thank-You Notes

No matter how big or small, expensive or not, every gift should be acknowledged with a written thank-you note. That's a handwritten note, not a preprinted card bearing your signature. Your guests went through time, energy, and money to present you with the gift. Give them the same respect in return. Write out each thank-you note. Both wife and husband should participate. After all, the gifts are for him, too. The notes don't have to be long and wordy, just polite. Each message should mention the gift

Every gift, no matter how small, should be acknowledged with a written thank-you note.

by name and say something about how it will be appreciated. For example,

Dear Mr. and Mrs. Smith,
Thank you so much for sharing our wedding day. It meant so much having you there. Thanks for the lovely blue blanket, too. It's just what we'll need for snuggling on cold evenings.

Sincerely,
Betty and John Brown

If the guest could not attend the wedding but sent a gift, acknowledge the thoughtfulness with such wording as,

Dear Mr. and Mrs. Smith,
We're so sorry you weren't able to attend our wedding. You certainly were in our thoughts and we appreciate your best wishes. Thanks for the beautiful toaster. You can bet it will get plenty of use and enjoyment.

Sincerely,
Betty and John Brown

A gift of cash could be acknowledged with a note reading:

Dear Uncle Ben and Aunt Bea,
John and I are so happy you were able to attend our wedding. Your generous gift will soon be put toward a television for our living room.

Never mention that the gift was the wrong color or of little use. Always find something nice to say about the gift, and always complete your thank-you notes within a month after returning from your honeymoon. Some etiquette "experts" may say you have up to a year to acknowledge wedding gifts, but how happy would you be if someone took 365 days to tell

© Cindi Kinney/The Stock Agency

you how much she appreciated your thoughtfulness or enjoyed your company?

Unless the guest is a close relative, always use your last name when closing the note. Guests may know more than one couple named "Betty and John." It's also an opportunity to let guests know if you are retaining your maiden name. Instead of signing the note "Betty and John Brown," sign it Betty Smith and John Brown." Guests will get the message.

Gifts from the Newlyweds

You'll be on the receiving end of most wedding-related gifts, but there are some that you will also give. Gifts to your attendants are a must. These are usually given at the rehearsal dinner. Nothing expensive is expected—here, it's the thought that counts. If you've ever been in a wedding party, you know how much you appreciated (or didn't appreciate) the gift that the bride gave you. Go with your instincts. The bride usually knows her attendants' likes and dislikes. You don't have to give every woman the same gift. If each has a definite personality, each can get a gift that is individually suitable. All gifts, however, should be about the same cost. You may want to give the maid of honor something extra special since she has extra duties to perform. The most popular attendants' gifts are earrings, necklaces, crystal or porcelain boxes, picture frames, bracelets, fragrances, figurines of bridesmaids, personal care appliances, and pins.

Every aspect of your wedding will be memorable, but make it fanciful as well. A carriage ride is a time-honored touch of romance. It's a storybook setting for photos, too, but be sure the carriage is spotless!

Look through old family photos and historical records for ideas to make your wedding even more meaningful. In this 1935 wedding, the groom, a speedway rider, whisked his new bride away on his motorcycle. Look for ethnic traditions, too. Search your heritage for a special song or dance that will add to the beauty and texture of your wedding day.

The groom's attendants should be given presents, too. The same rules apply: Give everyone the same gift or spend the same amount on more personalized gifts, with something extra special for the best man. The most popular gifts for attendants of the groom are mugs, pen and pencil sets, money clips, key chains, cuff links and tie bar sets, wallets, sports equipment, jewelry, personal care appliances, pocket knives, grooming kits, clocks, watches, and flasks.

It's also appropriate to give similar gifts to people who helped you on your wedding day, but are not necessarily attendants. These include special friends who helped you get dressed, made wedding plans, took care of the guest book or the gifts, or baked cookies for the reception, and those who participated in the ceremony but weren't hired to do so.

These might include guests who did readings, a soloist or musician, or acolytes. If the drivers of wedding party cars were friends who volunteered their services, they too should receive token-of-appreciation gifts.

It's getting to be more and more popular for couples to give each other special presents. This custom currently is practiced by 58 percent of all newlyweds. The gifts should be personal and lasting with special value. The most common choices for the groom to give the bride are jewelry, silver picture frames, or a silver-handled vanity set. For the bride's gift to the groom, the choices are jewelry, silver picture frames, a special paperweight, or other desk accessories.

Giving presents to the parents is also becoming popular. Often, something for the house as opposed

to the individual is chosen. Some gifts that are given frequently are porcelain vases, picture frames, photo albums, candy dishes, paintings, or other pieces of wall art. These are usually delivered immediately after the wedding or as soon as the couple leaves for the honeymoon.

Yet another form of gift-giving that's finding its way into more and more weddings is bestowing tokens of appreciation, or "favors," on guests. In some social circles, it's an expected tradition, in others it's a rarity. You know best. Should you decide to follow this idea, the items don't have to be expensive, but should be of some use. Ask your wedding consultant or retailer to make suggestions. Some favors that are given frequently are small boxes or sacks of candy, bookmarks, candles, small figurines, small bells, sachets, packages of potpourri, and small bud vases. Christmas ornaments are also common gifts. The most popular choice of ornament is a star or bell.

Protecting the Gifts

Weddings are happy times for most people, but can turn into sad events for some. An unfortunate fact is the amount of thievery that creeps its way into many of today's weddings. Professional thieves have been known to search the newspapers to find addresses of wedding reception locations or the homes of the bride, groom, or their parents. Thieves know that the homes of the wedding party's key members will be vacant for at least four hours. It will give them ample time to break in, take what they want, and leave without any worry of getting caught.

Many a bride has also found her wedding gifts stolen from the reception hall. Unscrupulous visitors posing as wedding guests or catering workers have been known to help themselves to the presents waiting to be opened after the reception. Too many couples have also come home to totally empty homes or apartments, because thieves not only knew where they lived but that they would be away for a week or more.

Security is a classic case of an ounce of prevention being worth a pound of cure. Be happy but be careful. If you must, hire security guards to watch your home during your honeymoon, and the home of parents during the wedding. A guard in plain clothes can also attend your wedding just to protect your gifts as well as the valuables worn by your guests.

If you can't afford outside security, ask special relatives or friends to serve security duty. Check with your insurance company, too. For a few pennies you might be able to buy a valuable insurance rider to cover losses related to your wedding and honeymoon.

For security's sake, be sure the local newspapers print nothing about your wedding until you are back from your honeymoon. To publish those details before the wedding or while you are still away on vacation can be asking for trouble.

CONSULTING A FLORIST

Flowers

*F*lowers have always been a part of weddings throughout the world. Yours probably won't be an exception to that lovely tradition.

Incorporating flowers into your wedding is a beautiful addition to a wonderful event, and only you can control the results.

Cost is one of the major factors. If cost is no concern to you, then order away! If it is, there are more economically conservative routes to take—all of which can enhance your wedding.

Before you even think of visiting a florist, check with the sexton or caretaker of the location at which your wedding ceremony will take place. If the event is in a church or synagogue, are there special regulations about flowers that must be met? Does the church or synagogue have a special commitment with only one florist? Must you use that florist for your church flowers? Ask before you end up with an unnecessary bill.

Ask the sexton or caretaker, too, if any other weddings are scheduled for the same day, or the day

before. If so, you may be able to share floral expenses with the other couples, and everyone saves money that way. If not, ask what the church or synagogue's regulations are on removal of flowers. Some places throw them out immediately after each ceremony. If this is a possibility, have an usher rescue the arrangements so they can be used at the reception—and save you money.

Ask the wedding planner at the reception site about floral arrangements, too. You might be paying for centerpieces as part of your overall package deal without even knowing it. There's no reason to order doubles. The reception hall or restaurant may also have nonfloral centerpieces, such as candle holders, which would work just as well—and cost you nothing. Ask!

CONSULTING A FLORIST

How do you find the florist that's best for you? Again, ask. Talk to friends who recently got married or who frequently use the services of a florist. Find out what they like best about the florists they use. Visit many of the area's florists, too. Ask to see samples of their work. If their designs are not what you had in mind, move on.

Most florists use design books created by floral suppliers to generate ideas. If the samples of one florist look very much like those of another, that's why. There's nothing wrong with that, if you don't have any special requirements. If you do, be sure the florist can handle them before signing any contracts. If there's even the slightest doubt in your mind about the florist's abilities, don't sign.

There's very little you can do to salvage your wedding flowers if the florist doesn't meet your specifications on the day of your wedding. You either have to use the wrong flowers or none at all. In short, you are at the florist's mercy. Do your homework and avoid any unnecessary risks.

With modern technology, just about any flower you want will be available any time of the year. However, if your choice of flower is not in season, or a flower is more unusual, cost can be a determining factor. Ask the florist to tell you about cost and availability of seasonal flowers.

Colors and Styles

You can have any color in floral form. If it's not the flower's natural color, it can be tinted to match your specifications. Your florist may also suggest mixing fresh flowers of natural colors with a few silks in designer colors to obtain the exact look you want. Go with it; you won't be disappointed. Remember that even though tradition has it that brides must carry all-white bouquets, you are free to carry whatever color you like.

The bride should always bring in a fabric swatch from her gown, the bridesmaids' gowns, her mother's dress, and any other outfit that she wants to match. Telling the florist that your gown is "ivory," that your attendants will be wearing "light pink," and that your mother will be in a "pastel blue," is asking for trouble. There are numerous shades of these and every other color.

You might even show pictures of the gowns to the florist, or bring in the gowns so he or she can get a feel for the style and decorations. You certainly don't want to carry bouquets that will hide the gown's most beautiful features.

If the gowns have plain skirts, the florist might suggest long, flowing bouquets. If the skirts are frilly or very decorated, small arm bouquets are best.

With hand bouquets, rest the arms at hipbone level. It will give the best overall look. Arm bouquets should rest in the crook of the arm. Baskets are held in one hand to the side.

A special word of advice: Instruct all attendants to carry their bouquets the same way. Having one holding her flowers as if they were made of lead and another up so high they could be an offering to heaven can ruin the look of the procession.

In addition to showing the florist dress colors and styles, provide details about the heights and weights of the women involved. If your bridesmaids are of various sizes, you certainly don't want a "one-bouquet-fits-all" situation. The standard size bouquet may end up looking like a tree if carried by a woman who is exceptionally tiny or thin, or an over-sized corsage by a woman who is large sized. Your florist should be able to make alterations to best suit each bridesmaid.

If you are having a flower girl in the wedding party, a basket of fresh flowers plus a small container of petals that she can sprinkle in front of you is needed. A ring-bearer will carry a flower-decorated pillow.

Ask your bridesmaids to make suggestions about the wedding flowers. The style of their dresses might be more appropriate with hair flowers, corsages, or arm bouquets instead of the traditional front and center bouquet.

Finally, remember that while carrying a bouquet may seem like one of the easiest things in the world to you now, it can be a challenge during the wedding when you are also juggling with a prayer book, gloves, and other accessories. If you intend to carry more than the bouquet, tell your florist in advance,

The traditional birth flower of the month list is:

January—carnation

February—violet

March—jonquil

April—sweet pea

May—lily of the valley

June—rose

July—larkspur

August—gladiolus

September—aster

October—calendula

November—chrysanthemum

December—narcissus
             (poinsettia is an alternative)

so it can be designed accordingly. Borrow a bouquet of artificial flowers and practice at home. Also practice with your maid of honor so she knows how to hold her flowers and yours when that time in the ceremony arrives.

You might also want to use the artificial bouquet for prenuptial photos. If so, ask the florist to provide you with one that is similar to your own flowers, so there will be a uniform look in the pre- and actual wedding photos.

Many brides often have their wedding bouquets duplicated in silk and use these for prenuptial photos as well as a keepsake for the happily ever after days.

Flower Choices and Meanings

Color will be the easiest part of your floral decisions. The next will be the selection of the flowers themselves. In addition to going with those of the season, you can give the wedding's flowers—especially the bridal bouquet—extra-special meaning. If the groom presented you with a particular flower during courtship, have it in your bouquet. A combination of both your birth months' flowers can also be a beautiful and personal symbol of unity.

Logistics

When's the best time to visit a florist? At least four months before the wedding is a safe time margin. During traditional wedding times, florists are very much in demand, and often have to refuse work if they are overbooked. Don't let that happen to you. Book your florist as far ahead as possible. You can always cancel the contract if you find a florist you prefer more, but you can't always sign up with the florist you originally wanted any time.

The florist will ask for the standard information, such as your name, address, phone number, place, time, and date of wedding. To cover all corners, give the florist your work as well as your home phone number along with those of the groom and both sets

of parents. That way there should never be an occasion when the florist can't reach anyone.

Your floral order should cover the ceremony, reception, the rehearsal hall, if necessary, and other locations, plus flowers for the wedding party. Ceremony particulars include alter flowers, pew markers, and a presentation bouquet for any special post-ceremony religious customs.

For the ceremony, the florist should also be able to supply you with kneeling benches, aisle runners, candelabras, a canopy, and any other special decorations you might want or need.

Your reception flowers should include centerpieces for each table—including a special centerpiece for the head table—plus cake decorations and favors for your guests if you so desire.

If the florist isn't familiar with the locations you selected for the ceremony and/or reception, insist that he or she visit them at least two weeks before the wedding to know the size and color schemes of

the rooms and any architectural details that could cause decorating problems. At the time the florist should also inquire about when he or she can set up the decorations and who should be notified about being let into the rooms in advance.

Flowers for Other Participants

Boutonnieres are the only flowers the men in the wedding party should have to handle. The groom's should match a flower in your bouquet. The other men should wear flowers appropriate for the wedding. Stems always go down.

A corsage is a corsage, right? Wrong! Don't order anything until you know the clothing styles to be worn by those who will be honored with corsages. Corsages can be pinned on a wrist or shoulder or used on a handbag, or as a hair ornament or even a waist accent. Let the wearer have some say in the corsage's details. Ask the florist for suggestions, too.

A single, long-stemmed rose might be just the right touch for a woman who is wearing a heavily beaded outfit. A large, elaborate shoulder corsage could be dazzling on a subdued colored dress with a draped collar. Be creative, but also be considerate.

Tossing the Bouquet

A tradition—dating back to the 1300s—has it that you should toss your bouquet to an unmarried girl before you leave for your honeymoon. That's also optional. Do it only if you so desire.

With wedding bouquets costing so much and having so much sentimental value, you may not want to toss your actual bouquet. If so, have the florist make up an inexpensive, smaller bouquet that can be tossed without any worry. The recipient will be just as thrilled.

Your florist might also devise a bouquet where the center is actually a corsage that can be worn for your honeymoon trip and the rest tossed to the crowd.

Other Floral Tokens

A final word about your wedding's flowers: There's often the question of what to do with all the flowers when the ceremony and reception are over. One solution is to give them away to your guests. Instruct the caterer to put a special mark on a coffee cup at each table. Whoever gets the marked cup gets to keep the centerpiece or has first refusal rights to it.

Another approach is to instruct the ushers to gather the centerpieces and arrangements and deliver them to the local hospital to be distributed to patients who haven't received any bouquets of their own, or to a local home for shut-ins and the aged. (Check with the hospitals and institutions in advance to see how and if they want to handle it.)

If someone very dear to you couldn't be at the wedding due to illness, a bouquet could be delivered to him or her. The flowers could also be put on the graves of loved ones as a way of sharing your special day with them.

The language of flowers isn't used very often anymore, but it still does exist. Carrying flowers that have meanings very special to you can make your wedding that much more personal and unique. Here are a few appropriate selections:

Camellia—perfect love

Carnation—lasting bonds of perfection

Chrysanthemum (white)—I love you
(yellow)—truth

Daisy—gentleness

Hyacinth—modesty

Ivy—fidelity

Lilac—humility

Lily—purity

Orchid—magnificence

Roses—love forever

Violet—modesty and meekness

Flowers are an important part of your wedding. As decorations and fashion accessories, they add color, beauty, and excitement every step of the way. Flowers are symbols of life. Share your flowers with those especially close to you. The blossoms can later be pressed or dried so they are long-lasting keepsakes.

DELICIOUS OPTIONS

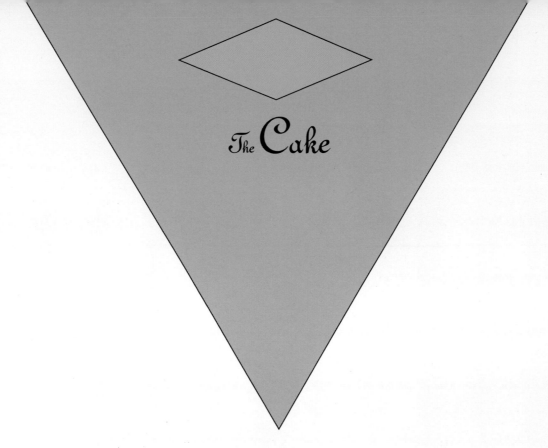

The Cake

Your wedding cake will probably be the most memorable food at your reception. The cake is also the most recognized symbol of a wedding—perhaps with the exception of two gold rings—and actually has quite a history. As far back as ancient Rome, weddings have featured some form of cake. In those days, loaves of barley bread were offered to Jupiter and then ripped apart over the bride's head to ensure her fertility. Over time, each country or geographic region eventually formed its own version of the wedding cake. In most of the world, the white frosted tiered cake is popular, but that shouldn't limit your choices. Investigate the customs of your ancestry. For a touch of originality, you might want to have a French *croquenbûche* or Swedish *fomekaken* in addition to the traditional cake. Note the use of the words "in addition to." Even though you might find having a wedding bread from your ancestors' Alpine village a charming touch, don't expect all the guests to share your idea. Have the bread for you, the groom, the wedding party members, and perhaps as an option for the rest of the guests.

Also have the more traditional cake, which will be most appreciated by your guests.

DELICIOUS OPTIONS

Why are most wedding cakes yellow or white and frosted with a white icing? Because it's the safest choice. Again, it's keeping your guests in mind. It would be difficult to find someone who didn't like a vanilla cake, or can't eat one due to health reasons. The same can't be said for other cakes—although you can have any type cake you like. Your baker should be able to handle any request, from carrot to chocolate, chocolate chip to applesauce. There are also no laws that insist your cake be frosted in white. If color coordination is an important part of your wedding picture, your cake can be frosted in the wedding's theme color or a combination of that color with white. It's your wedding. It's common, however, that cakes for second weddings be frosted in a pastel shade, especially pink.

If you want a chocolate, carrot, or a cake other than white or yellow but are concerned about the guests' tastes and dietary requirements, have the top layer —since the top layer belongs to you and the groom— done in a special flavor and the rest done in vanilla. That should make everyone happy.

Working With Professionals

If your wedding is being catered by a hotel or established banquet facility, most likely a cake is part of the overall package. Don't settle for that if you haven't tasted the kind of cake they expect to give you. The cake is too important a part of the wedding to be left to chance. Ask the caterer to provide you with a slice of the wedding cake or even a single-layer, small wedding cake that you, your fiancé, and parents can sample. If you don't like it, don't buy it. Have the chef try different recipes until the cake you get is what you want. If the chef can't or won't accommodate your request, get a reduction in

© J.B. Fairfax Press

Don't feel you have to have the traditional stacked wedding cake. These separate tiers—maybe different kinds of cake—are joined by satin ribbons.

the catering fee and buy your own cake from an outside bakery. While some caterers won't give you a lower price if you provide your own cake (since the price they gave you was a "package deal" and you turned down their cake by choice), hold your ground. No caterer is going to risk losing the entire wedding order or making you unhappy because of the cake. Caterers know that good word-of-mouth is their best form of advertising. If you want something they don't usually provide, mention it and work out a deal.

Size, Shape, and Decoration

Assuming you are going to buy the cake on your own, shop around for not only the best taste but also the best look and price. Visual impact is an important part of the wedding cake's presentation value. Tell the chef how many people you expect to have at

your wedding and ask to see photos or models of cakes. Remember, the wedding cake is the first thing your guests will see at the reception and the last thing they'll taste. It's that important!

If your friends or family are accustomed to taking a piece (or pieces) of wedding cake home with them —in addition to what they might have consumed at the reception—keep that in mind and tell the baker. You may have 100 guests at your wedding, but a cake serving 200 pieces may be the most realistic choice. Remember that round cakes are the most popular, but square cakes can give you the most pieces, and are easier to cut.

When ordering your cake, be sure to cover all the points: flavor of the cake, color and flavor of the frosting, flavor of the filling if there is to be any, colors of the decorations, and the topper. The variety of appropriate wedding-cake toppers in today's market is vast. Only settle for the plastic bride and groom

figurines or lovebirds the baker provides if that is what you want, but chances are you'll want something more original and of better quality. Shop at your local gift store. There are beautiful figurines of couples, doves, bells, and other wedding symbols that are perfect cake toppers and wonderful keepsakes. If you decide on a porcelain or glass sculpture, bring it to the baker at least two weeks ahead of time so he or she can be sure the cake's structure is strong enough to hold the object and can work out a decoration scheme to complement the special piece.

Special Considerations

Order your wedding cake at least a week in advance. Leave a deposit of 25 percent at the time, but be prepared to pay the entire bill the day of the wedding or before. No baker is going to leave the cake without full payment. Upon ordering the cake, give

Every wedding has a cake, be it a frosty mountain of sugar roses and silver frosting or a simple homemade pastry. The tradition of cake allows the couple to start life full of sweetness and the guests to leave the wedding with a sweet taste in their mouths. Select the flavor, size, shape, color and decorations you like best. Anything goes and everything's right.

the baker complete directions on how to get to the reception location and strict orders of when the cake should arrive and to whom the cake should be delivered. Leave nothing to chance. You will never forgive yourself—nor will your guests ever forget—if there is a wedding cake mishap.

If you want fresh-flower decorations on your cake, tell the baker the name of your florist so they can work out a decorating scheme. The baker might deliver the cake to the florist a few hours in advance or the florist might decorate the cake at the reception site. Whatever you want can be accomplished, just be sure to tell your plans to everyone involved. Be especially sure to tell the banquet hall manager or whoever is in charge of the reception, so there is

someone available to accept the cake—and have a proper table waiting for the prized pastry.

Depending on your budget, the wedding cake can be cut and distributed in small white boxes or bags at the end of the reception for guests to enjoy at home, or can be used as dessert at the reception itself. With wedding receptions being so costly, many couples are using the cake as the meal's dessert.

The First Anniversary Cake

The top layer traditionally belongs to the bride and groom. According to custom, it is to be saved and enjoyed on your first anniversary. However, modern standards have relaxed that rule. If you and your

groom may relocate and have no idea where you will be living a year from your wedding, you can enjoy the top layer as dessert for your first home-cooked meal or any other time the opportunity calls for a special touch of romance. Other options are to freeze just two pieces of the cake for the first anniversary celebration, or have the original baker provide you with a small wedding cake of the same recipe.

The Groom's Cake

Cost and tradition have also taken opposing sides when it comes to another wedding-related cake—the groom's cake. Tradition dictates that if the wedding cake is enjoyed at the reception, guests take home a boxed piece of the groom's cake to consume later. Tradition also says that unmarried women should put the piece of cake under their pillow the night of the wedding so they can dream of the man they will marry. So much for tradition.

Having a groom's cake is a lovely touch. It's memorable and can be costly, but then isn't everything involved with a wedding? The groom's cake is usually a dark, rich fruit cake, although in many cases chocolate is a suitable substitute. The wedding cake baker should be able to provide you with a groom's cake with very little trouble. But if that isn't the case, chances are there's a relative or close friend who would be honored to provide you with such a culinary delight.

In fact, that talented individual also may be able to provide you with a splendid wedding cake. It can add such a special, personal touch to that so very important part of your wedding.

Cutting the Cake

White or pink, vanilla or chocolate, round or square —whatever the cake may be, you and your husband will still cut the first piece. This can be easy or awkward. Practice will make all the difference…especially if your gown has sleeves that might get in the way. Practice cutting a cake both by yourself and with the groom. This rehearsal will come in handy later. Decide in advance if you will or will not feed each other the first piece—and how messy that feeding will get. Many a couple had their first argument at the wedding reception due to a surprise cake fight. If you are against such behavior, settle the matter before the wedding. Remember, all eyes— and cameras—will be on you and your husband when it comes to cutting and eating the cake. For posterity's sake, be polite.

Leave the rest of the cake-cutting to the caterer or close friend. If you intend to keep the top layer, let the person cutting the cake know in advance so that it is removed and handled with care before your guests are fed.

Classic Recipes

Just about every cookbook has a white or yellow cake recipe that can be increased to handle the amount of guests you expect. Here is the most popular white wedding cake recipe, suggested by the Wilton Company of Woodridge, Illinois, recognized as the world's leading supplier of cake decorating supplies:

White Wedding Cake

6 cups sifted cake flour
2 tablespoons baking powder
1¹/2 cups butter or margarine
3 cups sugar
12 egg whites
2 cups milk
1 teaspoon vanilla extract
Preheat oven to 325°F. Grease bottom of pans and line with waxed or parchment paper.

Sift together flour and baking powder. Set aside. Cream butter and sugar together until light and fluffy. Set aside. Beat egg whites until stiff but not dry. Set aside.

With mixer at slow speed, add flour mixture to butter mixture, alternately with milk. Beat well after each addition. Beat in vanilla extract.

Gently fold egg whites into batter. Pour into prepared pans. Bake until toothpick inserted into center comes out clean.

Yields: 12 cups of cake batter.

One recipe will fill 1 14-inch-round pan, and bakes approximately 50 minutes at 325°F. Check the batter chart on page 00 for other size pans.
Here's the most popular wedding fruitcake recipe, also courtesy of the Wilton Company.

Traditional Wedding Fruitcake

Firm and moist, this is perfect for decorating in the English style. Because of the richness,

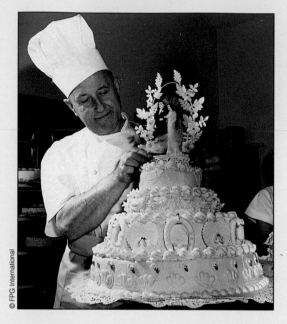

© FPG International

smaller slices are served. Keep this in mind when figuring servings.

3 cups all-purpose flour
2 teaspoons baking soda
1 teaspoon baking powder
¹/2 teaspoon cloves
¹/2 teaspoon nutmeg
¹/2 teaspoon cinnamon
¹/2 teaspoon salt
1 pound candied cherries
¹/2 pound mixed candied fruit
1 jar (8 ounces) candied pineapple
³/4 cup dates
1 cup raisins
1¹/2 cups pecans
1¹/2 cups walnuts
¹/2 cup butter
1 cup sugar
2 eggs
¹/2 cup apple or pineapple juice
1¹/2 cups applesauce

Sift and mix flour, baking soda, baking powder, spices, and salt.

Cut up fruit and coarsely chop nuts. Mix the fruit and nuts together. Cream butter and sugar. Add eggs and beat well.

Beating until blended after each addition, add dry ingredients and juice alternately to the creamed mixture. Mix in fruit, nuts, and applesauce.

Bake at 275°F about 2¹/2 hours.

Run a knife around sides of the pan and let cake set 10 minutes in pan. Remove cake and cool thoroughly. It keeps well for two months. It also freezes well, if wrapped tightly.

Fill 3-inch-deep pans two-thirds full. This recipe yields 9¹/2 cups of batter and will make one 10- by 3-inch cake.

Chocolate Wedding Cake

If it's a chocolate wedding or groom's cake you want, here's a recipe from the Wilton Company.

8 (1-ounce) squares unsweetened chocolate
1 cup butter or margarine
2 cups hot water
4 cups sifted cake flour
4 cups sugar
¹/2 teaspoon salt
2 cups sour cream
2 teaspoons vanilla
1 tablespoon baking soda
4 eggs, beaten
Grease, flour, and line pans with parchment or waxed paper.

Melt chocolate in the top of a double boiler over hot water. Combine butter and hot water in a saucepan. Bring to a boil. Stir in melted chocolate.

Sift together flour, sugar, and salt. Pour chocolate mixture into flour mixture all at once. Blend well. Mix in sour cream, vanilla, and baking soda.

Add eggs. Turn into prepared pans. Bake at 350°F, 30 to 35 minutes or until cake tests done. Remove from oven and cool pans on racks.

Yields: 10 cups batter. Makes 2 10-inch layers.

Additional Hints

- If you like to bake ahead, do so. Your baked cake can be frozen up to three months wrapped in heavy-duty foil.

- Always thaw cake completely before icing. Keep it wrapped to prevent it from drying out. Your cake will still be fresh and easy to ice because it will be firm. It will also have less crumbs.

- Packaged, two-layer cake mixes usually yield 4 to 6 cups of batter, but formulas change, so always measure.

A Handy Batter Guide

- One two-layer cake mix will make: 2 8-inch-round layers, 1 10-inch-round layer, 1 9- by 13- by 2-inch sheet, 1 mini-tier cake.

- If you're in doubt as to how many cups of batter you need to fill a pan, measure the cups of water it will hold first and use this number as a guide. Then, if you want a cake with high sides, fill the pan two-thirds full of batter. For slightly thinner cake layers, fill one-half full. Never fill cake pans more than two-thirds full. Even if the batter doesn't overflow, the cake will have a heavy texture.

- For 3-inch-deep pans, we recommend pound, fruit, or pudding-added cake batters. Fill pan half full only.

Courtesy J. B. Fairfax Press

HIRING A PROFESSIONAL

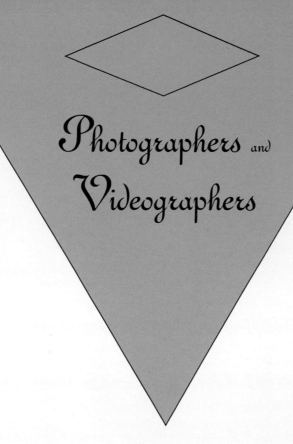

Photographers and Videographers

Chances are you know at least a dozen people with very good still and video cameras, and all are willing to make a record of your wedding. Let them—but also hire professionals. You can never have too many wedding photos or movies, nor should you rely on a novice—no matter how good his or her intentions—to take all the pictures you want at the quality you want. Photography is not the place to trim the wedding budget. These are the keepsakes you'll show to your friends and enjoy yourself over and over for years. If the budget is a matter of concern,

have a professional photographer do formal photos before and immediately after the wedding ceremony. Assign a few friends to take casual candids. This should give you a good selection for your album.

Before you smile for your first photo, there are many details that must be taken care of. First is to check with the minister or whoever will be performing your ceremony. Some ministers don't permit photographers to work during the ceremony—no matter how discreet they may be. The ministers feel the photographers distract from the meaning of the ceremony. If your officiant is of that mind and you want ceremony photos, change officiants.

Hiring a Professional

Select a photographer with as much concern as you put into finding the perfect dress, florist, or baker. Photography is a vital part of your overall wedding. Those pictures will be a lifetime investment. As such, shop for quality, not price. Look at samples, then look at more samples. Ask for the names and phone numbers of three brides for whom the studio recently worked. The best advice will come from a former customer. When you've found a photographer whose work you admire, then talk price. Chances are the photographer will have a "package deal." This can save you a lot of money, provided it gives you what you want. Know the costs of extra photos, enlargements, and all else before you make any written commitments.

Whether you select a studio with multiple photographers, or just one person, get to know the person who will be working at your wedding. If your personalities aren't compatible, ask for someone else. After all, you'll be spending a lot of time with that person on one of the most important days of your life. You don't want to spend the bulk of your wedding day being followed by someone you don't like. It will show on your face—and in your photos.

Contractual Considerations

When it comes time to finally write up the orders, ask the photographers to cover all the options in full details so both parties will know exactly what is available and what you want.

Find out if permanent proofs of the still photographs and videos or "roughs" must be returned within thirty days. If yes, do you get to keep the proofs at a later date? If not, what happens to them? Ask if you can buy them at a nominal charge. Also, find out when you get to see proofs or roughs and finished photos or tapes.

Points to cover with the still photographer include costs for quantities and enlargements of certain photos, a selection of albums for parents and key family members, and framed photos for members of the wedding parties.

Two other points you may want to cover are negatives and insurance. Most photographers won't part with their negatives, in hopes that you will order more photos eventually. If it's at all possible, obtain those negatives. Photographers tend to keep negatives for no longer than a year, but what happens five or more years after your wedding when the original photos may be fading or you want new copies for unforeseen reasons? Insist on owning the negatives. The other point is photo insurance. What happens if for any reason the photos don't turn out? Will the photographer pay for damages and costs to re-create at least the

wedding party photos? While nothing will ever take the place of the lost photos, you shouldn't be left in both financial and psychological ruin because of the photographer's or developer's errors or accidents.

Points to cover with the video photographer include sound. Will background music be dubbed on the tape? If so, do you select the music? What about credits? Can the names of the wedding's key members be listed on the tape? If so, will it cost you more? How about extra copies of the final tape? Are they available and at what cost? How much say will you have in editing the final tape? Are there any special effects you want—or don't want?

Again, it is your wedding. You should have final approval of everything. To the photographers, your wedding is just another job. To you, it's a milestone that can never be repeated.

© Bill Horsman

Photography Planner

When working with your photographer, leave nothing to chance. Together you should cover all possible points. Some to consider are:

- If you are going to have formal portraits done ahead of time, does the photographer have a dressing room in the studio where you can get ready? If not, can the photos be taken at another location where such facilities exist for your use? Does the photographer have a bouquet you can use for the prenuptial shots? When will the photos be ready for your approval and how soon after the wedding will they be available? Prenuptial photos should be taken at least a month before the wedding.

- If you are planning to send a wedding photo to the newspaper, obtain a list of requirements at least a month before the wedding so your photographer can provide the publication with exactly what is necessary. Most newspapers require black-and-white glossy-finish photos in a three-by-five-inch or five-by-seven-inch size. If all your photographer takes is color, you'll never see your photo in the newspaper.

- Require that the photographer visits your home, church, synagogue, reception hall, and any other wedding-related locations. The photographer should check for lighting, colors, and background and work out a set-up schedule at least a week before your wedding. This will also ensure that he knows where every phase of your wedding will take place and how to get there. If the photographer says there is no reason to visit, that he knows the places very well, watch out. He has no real interest in your photos, just your money.

- Your video photographer should do the same as mentioned above. Be sure both photographers work out a logistics understanding—put them in touch with each other in advance. You certainly don't want them fighting over the same angle at your wedding, nor do you want them to block the view of your guests. The photographers should also work out an understanding about lighting. One photographer's lights might ruin the work of the other. For example, you certainly don't want a videotape full of the still photographer's flashes, nor do you want still photos that were washed out by the video photographer's strong lights.

- If your photographer is planning on being at your service all day, does that person expect to be fed at your wedding reception? If so, be sure to make room for an extra person at one of the tables. Ask if the photographer(s) will have any assistants. Will you be expected to provide meals for them too? If the answer to all these questions is "yes," make a clause in the photography contract that you will be reimbursed for those meals and refreshments.

- If your wedding is going to have unusual touches, such as guest soloists or ancestral traditions, let the photographers know in advance so they will capture those special moments on film.

- If the photographers are also going to take candid shots, assign a close friend to act as guide and point out the most important or special guests so that they are recorded on film. Otherwise, the photographers might inadvertently dwell on some of the more striking-looking people in the room—who are distant relatives or others whom you were forced to invite.

- Be sure the video photographer is discreet with both lens and microphone. Catching a person off guard can cause lots of humiliation later. The classic example is the video photographer who left an open microphone on the head table to catch the wedding party's candid remarks and accidentally picked up an entire conversation about a bridesmaid's personal life.

- Chances are your still photographer will have a series of poses he puts everyone through and will tell you "everyone loves them." You are not "everyone." Thus, there's no reason why you should be expected to be treated like "everyone." If there are certain poses that you object to, don't do them. It's your wedding. The object of the photos is to give you a permanent record of the day, not to make you and/or your groom look foolish in ridiculous poses.

- Although your photographers will not be invited guests, they should be dressed as if they were. Most photographers will be dressed in regular business attire anyway, but don't leave it to chance. That goes for assistants, too. The classic horror story is that of the photographer who showed up in a proper business suit, but the assistant wore gym clothes.

- If your wedding is to be videotaped, be sure the photographer's sound equipment is sensitive enough to pick up the voices during the exchanging of vows. If not, all you will hear is the background music and a few guests coughing.

- Work out a timetable with the photographers so they know when to arrive at your home (and the groom's home, if you wish) and when they should be at the ceremony and reception locations. You'll have to live by those timetables, too. If you contracted the photographers up to midnight and at 11:55 P.M. you're not yet in the honeymoon travel outfit you want captured on film, they're not going to get the picture.

- The timetable should also include an approximation of when you will be cutting the cake, tossing the bouquet, enjoying your first dance together, and other rituals you want to have preserved on film.

The Wedding

*M*ost couples opt for a religious ceremony. Religious ceremonies are full of tradition, majesty, and splendor. They're also filled with rules that must be observed. These can vary greatly from house of worship to house of worship—even in the same religion! Other couples opt for more informal and nonreligious weddings. If you're still undecided on your choice of location, the information in this chapter should help you decide.

With the relaxation of traditional standards in many faiths, pastors, rabbis, and other religious leaders have been authorized to set codes and requirements that must be followed if a ceremony is to take place under their auspices. Some houses of worship require the bride and groom to attend prewedding religious instruction sessions, while others may even stipulate that the couple be of the same faith. Some require booking a year in advance; others require a month's notice. Don't take anything for granted. What may apply at one church or synagogue may not necessarily be the case at another. Also, the requirements set by one minister at a house of worship may not apply to all.

THE RELIGIOUS CEREMONY

If you intend to have a religious ceremony, contact your first choice of location as soon as possible. Speak to the pastor and ask about both church and individual rules and regulations. This is especially true if you would like to have a relative or friend who is not stationed at that church perform the ceremony. Many churches welcome outside ministers; some don't permit them under any circumstances.

If you find that a church or synagogue will not give you the freedom you want, or you cannot meet the particular requirements, go to another one of the same religion. You may require a letter of dispensation from your pastor, but there usually isn't any problem in obtaining such documents, especially if a donation is made.

The Vows

In its purest sense, a wedding involves the exchanging of promises between two people. The wording of those promises, however, is a different matter. Before you comb through books of poetry or write a plethora of pledges, ask whomever is to preside over the ceremony if any particulars have to be met. Some religious officials insist that the single set of vows sanctioned by that particular religion are spoken, others will give you more leverage as long as key phrases are used. Depending on the religion, a foreign language may also be involved. If such is the case with your wedding, practice reciting the vows for at least a week before the wedding. Otherwise the words the world is waiting to hear will come out garbled. If speaking in the foreign language is difficult for you, have the vows written phonetically. The words will flow and no one will ever know the difference.

Chances are the minister will give you a choice of three or more sets of approved vows from which to choose. With your fiancé, read them and jointly decide which will be used. Many churches and synagogues will not allow the bride to say one set and the groom another.

Names can be a tricky problem when it comes to religious ceremonies. Ministers will use whatever name you were given at birth, time of christening, or presentation at the temple. If it is a name you shed years ago, ask if the change can be made. Without giving it much forethought, many a bride or groom has had to face up to a first or middle name she or he hasn't used (or has kept a secret) for decades, much to the surprise of the guests.

THE READINGS

With every religious ceremony, no matter how large or small, there will be at least one reading. Often it is the minister's selection, read by him or her, but that's not always the case. Ask the officiant at least a month before the wedding how many readings you can have, from what selections, and if you can pick special friends and relatives to recite them.

Chances are the minister will allow anyone of the faith to do the readings. The maximum number of readings will probably be two, and at least one will have to come from a sanctioned text, most likely the Bible—and an approved passage at that. For all of its holiness, there are passages in the Bible that, no matter what the conditions, are just not appropriate for weddings. Rely on the minister to give you guidance.

© K. B. Kaplan/The Stock Agency

THE EXPENSES

Even if your wedding takes place in a monastery somewhere in the Swiss Alps, don't expect it to be a free ride. It costs money to keep a house of worship open—money you will be expected to donate. The amount depends on the circumstances. Some places charge according to your standing in the congregation. If you are a regular service-goer and donator, you may be asked to pay a minimum for use of the facilities with perhaps a stipend for the minister and whatever is the going rate for the number of altar servers you want, plus the fees for the organist, soloist, other musicians, and sexton. If you are not an established member of the congregation, the cost to

rent the facilities may be several times the member's fee, plus additional costs for services rendered. Ask the minister what you can expect in "suggested donation amounts." Don't even think of giving less than the suggestion. It simply is not acceptable.

Using your own minister doesn't exempt you from making the suggested donations. Many churches and synagogues have unwritten—but enforced—rules. A house of worship may expect you to pay the in-house minister even if he or she does not officiate, as well as pay for other "package-deal" services, such as the in-house organist and soloist, even if you do not use them. Inquire too if the fee to use the church or synagogue also includes time for rehearsal. Don't take it for granted. Churches and

synagogues have heating, lighting, upkeep, and personnel bills to pay. An extra hour for rehearsal means extra expenses all around.

Due to environmental reasons, it is not uncommon for houses of worship to have a cleanup clause in their agreement. It's similar to an apartment's security deposit. You may be asked to make a "clean-up" deposit just for safekeeping. If your wedding leaves the facilities in less than perfect condition, you might lose all or part of the deposit. The "conditions" range from removal of rice, confetti, and birdseed tossed by guests, cleanup of carpet stains, and payment for any damaged items, such as a planter knocked over by guests or the photographer in an effort to get the right angle.

Other Rules

Check with local law officials, too. What you might consider an innocent wedding ritual can be a criminal offense in that township. The two most prevalent wedding-related misdemeanors are throwing rice and flying balloons. More and more localities are banning such rituals due to environmental reasons. Birds can mistake rice for birdseed and die from eating it; balloons are unsafe if left to fly freely. This is especially true for mylar balloons or latex balloons with mylar streamers. Mylar can get caught in electrical lines and cause power failures.

Although it is your wedding, it doesn't mean you're going to have everything exactly your way—especially when it comes to a religious ceremony. When in church you are at the mercy of its laws, which also may apply to dress codes, music, and decorations.

Regarding dress, bare shoulders, bare backs, and low-cut necklines are often considered unacceptable. The same can be said for women wearing slacks and men not wearing ties. The church's or temple's standards should be respected. It is up to you to see that it is done.

During the ceremony, you may not be permitted to play "your song," especially if it is not linked to your faith. You may be required to select from a list of acceptable hymns or musical pieces. Such strictness went by the wayside in the late 1970s, but is coming back strongly as churches return to their fundamental regulations. Save that favorite song for the reception.

Your choice of decorations might also be limited. The church or synagogue might dictate that you limit your decorations to just a few bouquets of flowers—not the streamers and swags you always wanted. If you can't live by those rules, go to another house of worship that is more liberal with its regulations.

To prevent any misunderstandings, at the time of booking the wedding, ask an official to give you a complete set of guidelines that must be followed. Be sure they cover such topics as dress code, decorations, music, flowers, throwing of confetti, and the like. Plan your wedding according to those guidelines.

The Rehearsal

Unless your wedding is extremely casual, there are a number of procedures that will be part of the overall ceremony. One is a rehearsal. Depending on the demand for the site and availability of church personnel, the rehearsal can take place a week, day, or hour before the actual ceremony. Find out at least a month before the wedding so you can notify all wedding party members of their required attendance. Remember, even though you may be at the location for a rehearsal, it is still a house of worship and all rules of respect apply.

The purpose of the rehearsal is to familiarize you and everyone in your party with the location and what to do. If at all possible, have a musician perform the tune to which everyone will walk down the aisle. This

Weddings are full of tradition and rituals; participate in them all. You'll never have the chance again, and you and your friends will look back and savor every special moment. Make the most of your special day for it leads to a lifetime of special memories.

will help set the mood for the rehearsal as well as get everyone in step. The rehearsal should also include designated readers going over their parts and knowing how to use the building's public address system, as well as other participants walking through their roles.

No matter how detailed the rehearsal, there are bound to be snags. The object is to plan for as many potential problems as possible. If your gown has a long train, use a sheet or other piece of fabric as a substitute during the rehearsal. This will give you some idea of how to handle the train. It will also give your father, or whoever gives you away, an idea of how far back he should step to avoid walking on the gown. Members of the bridal party should also borrow substitute bouquets from the florist. During the ceremony, the maid of honor will have to hold your flowers as well as her own—this transfer of bouquets should also be practiced.

The rehearsal also provides the perfect opportunity to give the officiant the license and other legal documents that must be signed immediately after the ceremony. It also offers the chance for your father and the groom to pay for the use of the church and services without having to worry about getting all the right envelopes to the right people immediately after the ceremony. All payments should be in cash and in envelopes.

SEATING

Another important consideration for every ceremony is the seating arrangement. This can be done in many ways. Guests can be seated according to the time they arrive—first come, the closer to the altar— or according to their status in the family. If you opt for the second choice, there are two ways of handling it. One is to send a special "pew card" to those guests whom you would like seated in specially marked pews. The guests hand the ushers the cards and are immediately escorted to the marked seats. Another is to have a head usher who is very familiar with the family and knows important guests on sight.

While this can be chancy, since there is bound to be a special friend or relative with whom the usher is not familiar, it is still better than having ushers ask waiting guests if they are "special."

In the classic situation, all "general" guests are seated first. The immediate family comes next, with grandmothers and grandfathers being escorted to special seats. Then comes the mother of the groom with her husband. Finally the mother of the bride is escorted on the arm of the head usher. Once the mother of the bride is seated, no one else is escorted to a seat. It is time for the bridal party to make its entrance. Should any guests arrive after the mother of the bride is seated, they are expected to find their own seats via the side aisles. The center aisle is now considered "off limits." If guests arrive after the wedding party has walked down the aisle, they too are on their own and should find seats in the back of the room.

Guests in wheelchairs or who have walking diffi-culties may wish to be seated in the back of the room or in especially wide pews. Their special requests should be fulfilled, even if it means extra work for an usher.

Basic as it sounds, be sure seats are saved for the members of the wedding party! The first two pews on both sides of the aisle should be reserved for such purposes. Seats for the bride and groom should be placed at the altar.

The Guestbook and Register

Signing the guestbook is becoming a popular tradi-tion. Should you decide to do this at your wedding, be sure the ushers know how to handle it. Most likely, guests will be asked to sign it on the way into the ceremony. This is a nice custom, but it can cause a real bottleneck if many guests arrive at the same time. And you certainly don't want to have to wait an extra thirty minutes so your guests get a chance to autograph the book. The head usher should moder-ate the crowd for the signing of the book. Some sig-natures can be obtained before the ceremony, others

afterward while guests are waiting in the receiving line, or immediately after leaving.

The guestbook also should be available at the reception for the people who either missed a chance to sign it at the ceremony or didn't attend the ceremony.

Even more important than the guestbook, however, is signing the register—the official document that is filed with the government legally, making you husband and wife. This will only take minutes and is done immediately after the ceremony, usually in the sacristy or a side room of the church or synagogue. The minister will lead you through this pleasant task.

TRANSPORTATION TO THE CEREMONY

The old phrase "Get me to the church on time," is certainly a part of every wedding. With so many people and details involved, it's important that everyone, especially you and the groom, get there in plenty of time.

At least a few days before the wedding, time how long it takes for you to drive from your home to the place of the ceremony, and then from the ceremony location to the reception site. Now double that. It's best to have too much time than not enough. Give the doubled amount of time to the driver who will be responsible for taking you to the ceremony and the reception. No matter how long it takes to get from your home to the ceremony location, ask the driver to be at your front door at least thirty minutes ahead of schedule. This will allow time for an unexpected traffic jam and other factors, such as allowing the photographer to take photos of you and your parents getting into the limousine.

It's such an important day of your life, make every part of it a dream come true—even the transportation. Well-meaning friends might offer use of their automobiles, and driving the bride to the ceremony is an honor, but unless the vehicle can fit you in full gown and your escort next to you in comfort, it will

© Sandra Fisk/The Stock Agency

be a matter of thanks but no thanks. If the budget can afford it, rent a limousine for the day. If not, a large, spacious town car can be rented from any automobile dealer. Since your wedding will probably take place on a weekend, the rate most likely will be lower than you think. Take advantage of it. It is money well spent.

The bride and groom are responsible for providing transportation for everyone in the wedding party. Brand-new, matching rental cars might be the prettiest, and in the long run most cost-effective way to go.

If your wedding has a specific theme and another form of transportation might be more appropriate, consider it as an option, but do so realistically. For example, if your wedding has a country theme, you may long for a horse and buggy ride to church. While such a journey will be picturesque, how much room will the buggy provide for you and your escort? How will that buggy fare on the roads and in the traffic leading to the ceremony location? How do you feel about looking at the back end of a horse on your way to get married?

Before you hire drivers and rent automobiles for the wedding, notify all wedding party members of

your plans so they in turn can work out other transportation arrangements for their spouses, companions, or others who might be relying on them for transportation.

You'll find that centralization is the best way of getting the wedding party transportation situation handled quickly and easily. All of your attendants should be at your home at least forty-five minutes before the ceremony (fifteen minutes before any drivers). The male attendants should meet at the home of the groom at least an hour before the ceremony. All cars can be filled accordingly then and there. Remember though, ushers should leave first and be at the ceremony location at least thirty minutes ahead of time, ready to greet the first guest.

Whether or not you decorate your chosen form of transportation depends on a few factors. If the cars are rented, keep decorations to a minimum, such as a paper wedding bell tied to the radio antenna and beautiful bows tied to the door handles. If the car is privately owned, the extent of the decorations is up to the owner. Even the most minimal decorations should be placed with care, so as not to block the front window or mirror views of the driver or ruin the finish of the automobile itself. (Some shaving cream fades enamel paint; use whipped cream instead.)

Tying tins cans to the back of the wedding vehicle is an old custom. It originated in ancient times, when it was believed that weddings brought out evil spirits. The noise of the objects tied to the carts was meant to scare off evil spirits and bring the couple safely to their destination. Today, the noise is used strictly to catch attention from passersby—and embarrass the couple. Such objects are only tied to the car in which the couple will make their honeymoon getaway.

The custom of tying old shoes to the back of the car started the first decade of this century, when metal—including tin cans—was scarce and used for military purposes. Even at that time, country folk still believed in unseen evil spirits, and the shoes were meant to symbolically "kick" or "trip" such creatures —not to mention serving as attention-getters.

Whether a stately event at The White House or a family gathering in a backyard, every wedding is special in its own way. It is a time of sharing—sharing tastes and lifestyles, wishes and best wishes. Your wedding is special because of you.

© FPG International

Small-Scale Ceremonies

Many of the elaborate customs associated with contemporary weddings revolve around big, traditional affairs. However, if you have decided on a smaller, more intimate wedding, you can also incorporate a variety of traditions into the event.

The only ceremony that will limit your creativity is the one that takes place at city hall or in a judge's chambers. When such is the case, you are bound to the ceremony and procedures selected by the officiant. While it may not be grandiose, it can be a romantic—and less stressful—manner of getting married.

Logistics of At-Home Weddings

At-home weddings can be lovely, provided you keep the guest list and activities limited to what the location can comfortably handle.

Indoors or out, seating will be the most pressing problem. Before you comb the neighborhood for odd chairs, call a local party-rental-supply company. Your needs will be taken care of quickly and easily. Chances are the rental shop has handled many at-home weddings, whether they were informal or quietly elegant. Rely on that valuable experience for suggestions and advice.

If a party rental shop is not available, chairs can usually be rented or borrowed from funeral parlors, bingo halls, social clubs, or church groups. The cost of rental and quality of the chairs will vary. You will also be responsible for delivery to and from your home.

No matter where the wedding takes place, the bride's grand entrance is always an important and memorable moment. For at-home weddings, many brides make their entrances by coming down the staircase or entering from a back room. The bride should give herself that special moment, a chance for everyone to admire how beautiful she looks, and a chance for her to bask in the excitement of having all her friends gathered to honor her commitment to her bridegroom and his to her.

At-home weddings follow the traditional seating arrangements of the bride's and groom's mothers in honored locations, with close family members next in importance. Handling the wedding party will be the least of your problems as the informality of the event will call for simply a maid of honor and a best man.

Give your at-home wedding as much "bridal" atmosphere as possible. Flowers can decorate the staircase, tables, and front door. Music, even if played from a tape recorder, should fill the air to create the mood you desire.

For the at-home wedding, the officiant, whether a judge or minister, will handle all necessary ceremony paperwork and preparations. That does not mean, however, that you can't add personal touches.

If you and your groom wish to have a friend recite a special poem, then by all means arrange it. You also have the ultimate freedom to recite your own vows, but notify the officiant in advance so as not to catch him or her off guard. You might also want to present the officiant with a copy of your vows a day or two before the wedding just to make sure they cover all legalities.

Guests at a home wedding won't expect you to pull out all the stops as might be the case at a more formal affair. However, you should still have some refreshments, and definitely a wedding cake. To most people it just wouldn't be a wedding without it.

OTHER OPTIONS

Intimacy can make a wedding so special. If that's the quality you most desire, consider a very small wedding with the two of you surrounded only by close friends and family members. It will eliminate the need for much preparation and pressure. Such a ceremony and reception can take place just about anywhere—in a home, at a restaurant, or in a park. "Small" and "private" are the key words. However, you might still want to send out announcements to friends and other relatives. The same can be said if the wedding ceremony involves just the two of you, two witnesses, and an officiant. You are married and should notify everyone of the important step in your life. Under any and all circumstances, send announcements. Be they engraved or written by hand, it is a proper and polite procedure to follow. And for even the most intimate of affairs, have photos taken. This is a milestone that should be preserved on film.

If you had a small private wedding and the time comes when you wish your affair had been larger, there's nothing to stop you from renewing your vows in front of everyone you've ever known in the biggest room the world has ever seen, followed by an enormous reception. It's a celebration of love, no matter if it takes place a month, a year, or fifty years after the original ceremony.

The Reception

*T*he most logical way to begin planning your reception is to visit possible banquet locations. Inspect facilities and get sample menus and price guidelines. Also, learn if the places offer package deals. Armed with such data, you can determine approximately how many people you will want or need to have at your reception and start eliminating some of the location possibilities due to the size of the room. When looking at room sizes, separate the sales pitch from reality. The literature and salesperson might say that the room can "comfortably seat 200." Chances are that's theater-style, which means just rows of chairs. The room hasn't been considered for tables, a dance floor, receiving line, and other necessary space requirements.

Remember to ask as many questions as possible— for example, find out how the banquet hall defines "comfortable seating." Find out how many people are accommodated per table at a sit-down dinner. Six is preferable, but eight is maximum. Ten is way too many. Should you mention 200 people and the salesperson says 20 tables, start walking.

If your reception is going to have 200 people, don't settle for a room that can handle any less than 250 people. That should give you some elbow room.

Once you have the list of rooms down to a reasonable selection, look at price—better yet, inspect price. A dollar at one place may not necessarily bring you the same thing at another. When you've limited the selection to a handful, you should have a general idea of what your wedding reception will cost per head. Now you are ready to take money into consideration.

Covering the Expenses

Tradition dictates that the bride's parents pay for the entire reception. In today's economy, that is rarely the case. It's become quite common for both sets of parents to pay equally for the wedding or divide the costs according to finances, the number of invited guests on each side, and other deciding factors, particularly with regard to the reception.

The parents are most likely to pay for the reception if the bride or groom is still living at home, is still financially dependent on the parents, or is an only child. If, however, the bride and/or groom is financially independent and has not lived under the parents' roof for more than a year, it is not uncommon for the parents to turn over the cost in whole or part to the couple. However you work out the expenses, whoever pays has final say over particular details.

A wedding can be as costly or uncostly as you wish...and the budget allows. Often, the same wedding location can vary in cost due to month, day, and time. It's the law of supply and demand. Saturday evenings during June and August are the most popular times for wedding receptions. The demand drives up the cost. If finances are a concern, find out what the difference would be if you moved your wedding to an "off-season" month or an "off-peak" time. During a slow time, the establishment is more likely to work with you on price. The difference could be as much as 25 percent! Costs can also vary according to where in the reception site you hold

© Arthur Tilley/FPG International

Rely on your family and friends for advice in every matter of the wedding. Everyone will gladly share their opinions and experiences. And honor those especially close to you by seating them in places of honor, giving them special flowers to wear, or toasting them in return for their kindness, caring, and love.

your party. A second-floor or basement-level room could be 10 percent lower in cost than having the reception in the "main" floor room.

Go through all the estimated costs with a fine-tooth comb. Look for options and hidden costs. What the reception manager might call a "complete package" may not be what you consider a complete wedding. Have everything spelled out. Some pitfalls to watch out for are:

- Does that "deal" include enough service to handle your guests properly?
- Does the cost include taxes and gratuities? If so, at what percentage? Without looking, you might be charged a 30 percent gratuity.
- When the deal says "music," does that mean a live band? If so, how big is the band? Can you hear the band play at least a month before the wedding and get money back if you choose not to use it? Or does "music" mean a record player and a disk jockey?

- What denotes an "open bar"? Is it all beverages or just setups? Does it include tips for the bartenders, or will your guests be confronted with signs that say "tips" pasted to a large glass bowl?
- Are such considerations as parking, coat checking, and decorations included?
- Are the washroom facilities sufficient? The rest rooms should be big enough to handle any demands caused by your guests.
- Parking should be nearby and safe.
- Exits should be plentiful, well marked, and easy to reach. Check the building's inspection reports for safety and health. If there's an elevator, make sure it's in proper working order, too. Should these documents not be readily available, a call to the local licensing and inspections department will provide you with the data you want.

A reception is a costly affair. It's an investment—and one that can't be brought back for adjusting if all doesn't go well. It's now or never. Proceed with caution and lots of questions.

OUTDOOR FESTIVITIES

Garden weddings and receptions are lovely, but are subject to the whims of the weather. Never book a reception in an outdoor location unless the affair can be moved indoors if it becomes necessary.

A compromise is to set up a formal tent. For summer weddings, it provides a nice canopy to shield guests from the sun. A tent with a temperature control (heater or air conditioner) is the best selection—although tents with open sides should suffice under most circumstances. Toilet and washing facilities should also be kept in mind when planning an outdoor wedding—some municipalities actually require rental of portable toilets for large outdoor events. Also, rooms with privacy where the bride and groom can change into honeymoon outfits are essential.

THE RECEIVING LINE

Whether the reception is indoors or out, in your home or the White House, a receiving line will be a necessary element. The purpose is to give each guest an opportunity to congratulate the bride and groom, and for them to greet each guest. Whereas the receiving line after the ceremony will consist of the couple, female attendants, and both sets of parents, this does not necessarily have to be duplicated at the reception. A line of the bride and the groom and both sets of parents is equally acceptable.

Be ready for lots of hugs and kisses and compliments. Be ready to give a lot back, too. Guests will give you their wedding gifts as they come through the receiving line. To save time and trouble, ask the maid of honor and/or best man to stay close by to take the boxes from you and to keep any envelopes in a safe place. Appoint that person as the keeper of the gifts, and ask him or her to deliver the presents to your parents' home after the reception or to your own home after the honeymoon.

SEATING

Taking care of seating arrangements is a difficult task, but it must be done. Tradition says that the two most important tables are the "bride's table" and the "parents' table," but tradition has a way of being sidestepped. The classic bride's table consists of the couple in the center, with the groom at the bride's right. To the bride's immediate left is the best man, followed by an alternating line of half the bridesmaids and ushers. To the groom's right are the maid of honor and the alternating ushers and bridesmaids.

The classic parents' table consists of both sets of parents, the clergy member, and immediate family members who are not in the wedding party. The reality of divorces, remarriages, and other circumstances, however, might dictate a departure from tradition. If either set of parents is divorced and not on speaking terms, especially if a remarriage is involved, you may want to have a few "tables of honor" instead of one parents' table. Sit the parents and their new spouses at various tables along with close family members and special friends. If the clergy member is going to attend the reception, extend that invitation to include a spouse or friend. They too can be seated at one of the designated "special tables." Taking these simple precautions

Reception Planning Timetable

Timing will be an important part of your wedding reception, from the planning stages right down to the tossing of the bouquet. Start looking for the right reception location as soon as possible. A year in advance is not too soon.

At least six months prior to the wedding:

- Leave deposit with reception location

- If location does not provide all services, book:
  A. Caterer(s) (You may need more than one due to religious or dietary requirements)
  B. Musicians
  C. Baker

At least three months prior to the wedding:

- Complete guest list

- Select decorations for reception

- Order favors or special accessories for reception

- Order extra bouquet for tossing (if you will not toss your own flowers)

At least two months prior to the wedding:

- Finalize all reception plans, with the exception of the actual number of guests.

- Give the caterers a ballpark figure so they know how much food and preparation is necessary. The final head count won't be due until a week before the wedding

One month prior to the wedding:

- Work on seating plans for family and friends whom you know will be at the reception

- Complete seating for head table

- Plan receiving line

- Go over plans with photographer and band to make sure you get what you want

- Practice waltzing together. If neither one of you knows how, take a few lessons. Your first dance should be smooth and lovely

Two weeks prior to the wedding:

- Complete seating arrangements

- Have favors ready to go

- Verify all details with caterer, florist, band, and all reception service people

- Bride should practice dancing with her father

- Groom should practice dancing with bride's or his own mother

One week prior to the wedding:

- Give caterer and all food-related managers your final head count

- Notify family members and special guests of their table numbers so they won't get lost in the crowd

can make the day run much more smoothly.

If many members of your wedding party are married and would prefer to sit with their spouses rather than at the bridal table with their wedding partners, changes can be made here, too. An equally appropriate bridal table can consist of you and the groom, both sets of parents, the best man and maid of honor, plus any wedding party members who choose not to sit with their spouses or significant others.

The object of the seating arrangement is to make everyone as comfortable as possible. When it comes to setting places for friends, keep in mind their interests and ages. Mix people who would have common interests. You'll want to encourage conversation.

Other things to keep in mind when arranging seats are physical constraints (people with walking problems should not travel the length of the room to get to a table); young children (will they sit with their parents or will you have a children's table?); guests who have to leave early (put them all at the same table near an exit); and traffic flow to the dance floor, bar, and rest rooms. Also remember when numbering the tables, do so in a standard orderly fashion. Scattering the numbers throughout the room is asking for confusion.

SELECTING THE MEAL

Food is foremost in everyone's mind when it comes to receptions. There are, of course, many choices, so you may wish to narrow the possibilities to one of three basic approaches. The first is to serve fowl as the main entrée, be it chicken or turkey. It's the overall safest choice. Another is to give guests the option of having fish, fowl, red meat, or all vegetables. They can note their selection on the Rsvp form. This will take time to coordinate, but you may find it worthwhile. Each place setting will have to be marked with the person's entrée choice so the waiters will know what to serve to whom. A third alternative is to have a buffet. While this method is considered to be informal, it offers a wide selection of foods, so that everyone can get what is personally preferred.

Of course, other considerations factor in the choice of reception food. You'll have to draw up a budget—not only for food, but for liquor as well—and plan everything within the guidelines. You may have to modify the menu to suit religious customs of guests. For example, you may need to have two menus—one kosher and one general. At ethnic weddings, some couples supply a general menu and another featuring national cuisine—although the two always can be mixed.

The Time of Day

The menu and overall tone of the reception will vary according to the time of the day. A breakfast reception should be held from sunrise to 11 A.M. A brunch can be served from 11 A.M. to 1 P.M. A full luncheon can be held from noon to 2 P.M. A tea reception can be held from 2 to 5 P.M. A cocktail buffet reception can be held from 2 to 6 P.M. A dinner reception can be held from 6 P.M. onward.

Generally speaking, the later the reception, the higher the cost. For example, a breakfast reception certainly wouldn't have an open bar or dance band. A luncheon reception might include light alcoholic refreshments, while a dinner reception will include the complete open bar, dance band, and other formal trappings.

Service fees also are higher the later the reception is held. This stands to reason, as a breakfast or luncheon reception is informal and a buffet is very appropriate. An evening reception generally requires more service stations if a buffet is served, or more waiter or waitress service if a sit-down evening meal is served, because there are more courses. Should the caterer suggest "French service," this means one waiter or waitress is assigned to each table. It means the maximum in service —and cost.

A tea reception is generally the most cost-efficient. Light refreshments such as tea sandwiches and spreads, coffee, tea, juices, and champagne are appropriate fare.

The cocktail party reception relies more on drink than food. As such, it can be more costly than you might originally expect. While a cocktail reception may consist of just a selection of wines and champagnes along with finger foods and light desserts, the brands of the alcoholic beverages being poured can make the difference in expenses. You'll have to work out the details with your caterer. The rule of thumb is one drink per person per hour. A reception for 100 people should require about a case and a half of alcohol per hour.

Choice of Caterer

A caterer must meet your requirements on a number of factors, including price, food, location, and availability. Even the most delicious food won't leave guests with a pleasant taste in their mouths if the service is bad, so be sure that the caterer is the right choice for you.

Once you've narrowed down the list of possible caterers on price and selection, ask to sample some of their dishes. Caterers who really want your business shouldn't have any problem with this. Most

likely they'll ask you to visit their kitchens while they are preparing the foods for another affair with selections similar to those you are considering. If you are happy with the cuisine, ask about service. How much of a staff will be on duty for your wedding? If your reception is to be a sit-down affair, there should be a server as well as a busboy for no more than every two tables. There should be staff working during the cocktail hours, making sure all the foods are being replenished, as well as enough cleanup people to make the chore quick and easy.

Catering help should wear uniforms that are in keeping with your wedding. If you are having a formal affair, servers should be in black suits with white shirts and black ties. If you are going more casual, settle for just dark-colored pants, white shirts, and ties.

Caterers, like most businesses, are always looking for new customers. Unless you are very agreeable, be sure the caterer doesn't use your wedding as a sales pitch for other business. With this in mind, make sure someone keeps a close eye on business cards being left around the reception site—caterers have been known to do this.

Music and Dancing

Just because a band comes with the hall, it doesn't mean it's the band you want. Audition the band and talk to the bandleader. Consider the ages and tastes of the guests who will be at your wedding. The music should be varied enough to give everyone a few favorite selections.

When auditioning the band, present the bandleader with a list of tunes you want played at the wedding. Ask the band to play one or two. If it's not what you want, then don't hire them. It is better to go out and hire a band (and get money back from the hall) and pay a little more than to get stuck with a house band that doesn't meet your musical expectations. If the affair is more informal, you may prefer to hire a pair of musicians or even one musician.

Should you opt for prerecorded music, you may wish to hire a disk jockey. Ask to see the selection of records; you can always modify the choices to suit your tastes exactly. For very formal events, you may even opt for a selection of prerecorded music played without a disk jockey.

Whether you use a live band or recorded music, a timetable should be worked out. Select what you want played during the cocktail portion of the reception, during dinner, and then for dancing. If you don't work out such a schedule, the band could play a great dance number just as the entrée is being served and all your dancing friends will come back to cold food.

Tradition has it that the bride and groom have the first dance. Be ready. This is a very romantic time, and all eyes will be on you. Even if you have a favorite song that has the best upbeat tempo in the world, save it for later. Your first dance, captured on film, should be romantic. A waltz makes the best picture. If you don't know how to waltz, have a knowledgeable person instruct you or take lessons. The results will be well worth it.

Practice dancing with your father and father-in-law, too. The groom should do the same with the your mother and his mother. Those first dances are

© Mary Ann Evans

the centers of attention. Make people remember them for their beauty, not folly.

Every bandleader has a stock-in-trade selection of "first dance" songs. If you don't say anything, you're going to be dancing with your father to the tune of "Daddy's Little Girl," while your groom dances with his mother to the strains of "Boy of Mine" or "Sonny Boy." Both tunes are appropriate for the occasion, but are not the only choices. A waltz to classical music is just as suitable—and a lot less schmaltzy.

The look of the band and the disk jockey will be just as important as the sound. As with the caterers, be sure the musicians are dressed appropriately for your wedding, and that they don't give your guests sales pitches. There's no reason why the band should blanket your reception with business cards.

TOASTING TRADITIONS

Whether your reception is one of champagne or soft drinks, there are bound to be a few toasts. Traditionally speaking, the best man makes the first. He should ask your guests to join him in wishing the newly married couple a lifetime of happiness. A second toast can be made by the bride's father, welcoming her husband into the family and wishing everyone good health. The groom's father can welcome the bride into his family and also wish everyone good health. That usually concludes the formal toasts; afterward, anyone and everyone can make a toast.

When the toast is in honor of the two of you, stay seated and smile. And don't drink to toasts in your honor; you accept everyone else's respect. Only when the toast is for someone else should you stand and drink.

A nice gesture is for the groom to toast the lovely bride, thanking her for being his wife. He also should thank her parents (or whoever is hosting the wedding) for the wonderful reception. The bride does not return the toast to the groom. She sits during his toast, then thanks him when he sits down.

While every guest expects to participate in a few toasts at every wedding, there are different ways of getting their attention. These include the best man tapping the stem of his water glass with a piece of flatware to yelling for everyone to give him their full attention. These may be effective, but are certainly not the most polite ways to conduct such matters. The ringing of a bell is much more polite—and original. On the wedding table, near the best man, be sure to have a glass bell. He can ring this and get everyone's attention. You can keep the bell as a memento.

OTHER RECEPTION CUSTOMS

If the minister who officiated at your wedding also attends the reception, it is customary to ask him or her to recite a prayer before the main meal. Chances are many of your guests will not be of the same religious persuasion as you and the minister. So no one is uncomfortable, ask the minister to keep the prayer one of general thanks and brotherhood, not denominational. The minister should understand and behave accordingly.

Tradition has it that before the wedding is over, you should provide your guests—at least the unmarried ones—with mementos, namely the bridal bouquet and the bride's garter. As contemporary and fun as these customs may be considered, they can be traced to less civilized roots. Hundreds of years ago, it was considered good luck for guests to leave the wedding with something worn by the bride. At first, the bride would offer her handkerchief or other accessory, but as guests got rowdy and receptions got larger, well-wishers would often tear off a piece of the bride's gown. This eventually made the bride

scurry for safety. The couple would hide from their guests and appear on a balcony, toss the bouquet and a few other personal items, and run away before anyone could catch them. Thank goodness that custom has been refined.

Today, the object of tossing the bouquet is to bring some unmarried woman the good luck of being the next bride. The tossing of the bride's garter (by the groom) brings luck to an unmarried man so he will be the next man to wed.

You certainly don't need to follow any of these customs. If you decide to toss flowers to the crowd, it doesn't necessarily have to be your real wedding bouquet. If you want, save it as a keepsake for yourself and toss a small nosegay instead. It will serve the same purpose without you giving up such an important part of your wedding. The same can be done with the bridal garter. If you don't like the custom, don't participate in it. If you do, then wear two garters, one to keep and one to throw.

It's become popular in some cultures for the groom to wear a garter as well as the bride and throw it to the crowd. It is tossed to the unmarried women in addition to the bride's bouquet.

The tossing of the garter(s) and the bouquet usually signifies the end of the reception. If you are leaving for your honeymoon directly from the reception, throw your guests the tokens of good luck after you have changed into your traveling clothes. This will allow everyone an opportunity to give you and the groom one last toast of honor.

Leaving the reception is a milestone unto itself. It really signifies the start of your married life. But before you leave, take care of a few last minute details. Be sure someone will pack your wedding dress and bring it to the cleaner or other location you wish. Someone should bring the groom's tuxedo back to the rental place or wherever he wants. The florist should be ready to deliver a "thank-you bouquet" to parents the next day, in appreciation for the lovely wedding. Additionally, transportation should be waiting to take you away to the first stop of your honeymoon.

TRAVEL AGENTS
HONEYMOON ESSENTIALS

The Honeymoon

*N*owadays, the honeymoon is considered to be a vacation full of love and excitement. But there was a time when it was not so carefree an event. During the Greco-Roman period, the groom would "capture" the bride and cart her off to an unknown location so as not to be found, or "saved," by her relatives. During that time, usually thirty days—from new moon to new moon—the couple would drink a mixture of wine and honey. Thus the term "honeymoon." The bride was at the groom's beck and call. According to today's standards, this may sound harsh to say the least, but remember, in those times, the bride was considered the groom's property and could be handled however he wanted. Happily, whatever goes on during today's honeymoons is by mutual agreement.

It's estimated that about 75 percent of first-time married couples take honeymoons. The average honeymoon lasts a week and costs at least 1,500 dollars. That cost covers transportation, lodging, food, entertainment, and personal and gift purchases.

Courtesy of Jerry and Elka Levinrad

Start planning your honeymoon as soon as you book your wedding date. Those plans should begin with a discussion of what both of you want in a honeymoon. Make a list of categories, such as, beaches, mountains, city-sightseeing, a cruise, amusement parks, hiking, camping, big-name entertainment, swimming, skiing, and the like. So you both are totally honest, make your lists separately and then compare. Neither of you should "settle" or give in to an "anywhere you pick is fine with me." This is a once-in-a-lifetime event and your first chance to share everything life has to offer. Plan it together.

TRAVEL AGENTS

When you have the basic outlines of what you want in a honeymoon, work out a spending plan. This is different from a budget. A budget is too rigid. The spending plan will give you more options—plus hold some money in reserve for unexpected purchases or expenses.

Armed with a basic outline and spending guide-lines, visit a full-service travel agency. Traditionally, the larger the agency the better, as it tends to be on top of special deals and package plans, more so than smaller agencies, which may not have that much clout with airlines and hotels. The agent will make recommendations, lots of them. Listen closely, pick up all the brochures, and consider your options. You may have to give in a little here and there to get the best price for what you want, but it could be worth the difference. Look out for hidden catches, too. If a deal sounds too good to be true, it probably is.

Air Travel

Airfares vary greatly, depending on the airlines and the day and time of travel. Most airlines have the lowest rates for passengers flying on Saturdays and have purchased their tickets at least thirty days in advance. Ask the travel agent about such deals. If your wedding plans don't permit you to leave on Saturday, ask if you can fly at a special rate setup for a convention the agency might be handling. Only under extreme circumstances should you have to pay full coach fares. If that comes about, ask how much it is for a standby upgrade to first class. Some airlines will allow you to move up for as low as $20. It all depends on the airline and availability of first-class seats.

Airlines are famous for using language that sounds like double-talk, and that's exactly what it is. The travel agent might tell you the flight is "direct." Then suddenly after flying for one hour of a three-hour flight, you find yourself sitting at a different airport for an hour only to take off again, surrounded by different people. Confused, you ask the flight attendant, "Isn't this the *direct* flight?" She or he answers, "Yes." Still in a confused state, you ask, "But why did we stop?" Watch out for the answer: "This is a *direct* flight, not a *nonstop*." There's the airline double-talk. "Direct" means that the plane will eventually get to your desired destination without you having ever to switch planes. It does not mean that you will go *directly* to that destination without stopping. You might have one, two, or more stops to make along the way, but you will get where you want to go eventually. A "nonstop" flight is just that. There are no stops between the location from which you leave and your destination. Direct flights cost the same as nonstops, and they also fly more frequently. If your schedule can handle it, go for the nonstop.

Ask for special seating, too. The travel agent should be able to show you a chart of the plane's seating pattern. If the plane will fly over beautiful scenery or famous landmarks, you certainly don't want to have a great view of the wing. If legroom is important to you or your groom, ask for a seat at the bulkhead, or at least on the aisle. Be sure your seats are together, too. Just because your seat says Row Eight, Seat C, and his says Row Eight, Seat D, doesn't mean that there won't be an aisle between you. The travel agent might have thought that both of you wanted aisle seats, thus the aisle running between you. Leave nothing to chance.

Cruises

A cruise might be your idea of the perfect honeymoon, but make it as ideal as possible. Book early— the best cabins sell first. Ask the travel agent to show you photos or illustrations of the cabins on the ship you will be taking. Be sure everything is to your liking, such as a window cabin or not, full bathroom or just a shower, the level you want, and other important considerations. If not, you could find that "bargain" gave you bunk beds in an "inside room" —meaning no window or porthole—with just a toilet and use of a shower that's down the hall.

If you decide on a cruise, but have never taken one before, be safe instead of sorry. Visit your doctor and get preventive seasickness treatment. It will consist of a small medicated patch to be worn behind your ear, inside your elbow, or in some other inconspicuous location. Ask the doctor about sun block, too. Chances are you'll need it if getting a tan or at least spending a lot of time in the sun is part of your agenda. Play it safe: A good sun block will help you get a gradual tan or none at all.

When booking the cruise, your travel agent will ask you about meal seating—that means the time at which you prefer to dine. Most cruises have two seatings for each meal, an hour and a half apart. Breakfast might be served at seven and eight-thirty, lunch at eleven-thirty and one, and dinner at six and seven-thirty. Chances are you'll be better off at the later seatings. Families with children usually take the earlier seatings, as do senior citizens and conventioneers. The waiters are usually calmer at second seatings, too, knowing that they don't have to get you in, fed, out, and have the table ready again all in ninety minutes.

You'll also be asked about your seating arrangements, that is, if you would like a table for two or a table with other people for all of your meals. Whatever you prefer is up to you. You might want to ask if there are any other honeymooners on the cruise with whom you can sit. You're likely to have more in common with them than most other passengers.

Car Travel

If the honeymoon consists of traveling by car to your destination, you'll have the most freedom possible. Ask a travel agent or automobile club representative to work out a scenic route if that's what you desire, or the quickest route, if you prefer. The agent can also give you pointers about the hotels, shops, and other services or attractions you might pass. Also ask the agent about special car rental deals that could save you money.

Hotels

Hotels are more than just places with beds. They can also be minicities connected to shopping centers, convention centers, resorts in the middle of nowhere, and anything else you can imagine. Before you book a hotel, read the brochure the travel agent gives you, and then call the town's visitor and convention information bureau for more literature. If you are convinced it's the hotel you want, before you make any reservations, call the hotel itself and ask questions about the accommodations. Find out if there are any specific package deals available to save you money. Find out if conventions or other events will be going on during your intended stay that could create a noisy or otherwise unpleasant atmosphere. Make sure that no remodeling of major facilities will be underway. Not only might the construction be noisy, but you might also be denied use of the hotel health club, restaurant, or other facilities.

Be sure the hotel is everything and has everything you want. After you book the hotel, call it yourself and tell the concierge you will be on your honey-

© Michael A. Keller/FPG International

moon. You may be able to get a room upgrade at no extra charge.

No matter where you go or how you get there, plan as much in advance as possible. Contact the visitor's bureaus or chambers of commerce of each location and get a list of special events that will be going on during your honeymoon. If a special theatrical event is scheduled, you'll have to book your seats months in advance, and there's no way of knowing it unless you are told well ahead of arrival. If the location has no visitor's bureaus or chambers of commerce, the hotel's concierge should be able to provide you with a list of activities and events at least three months in advance of your arrival.

Honeymoon Essentials

Clothing is a major part of every honeymoon. What you wear in your bedroom is your own business, but what you wear in public can depend on a number of factors, such as weather and local customs. Rely on your travel agent for pointers on what both of you might wear and what is acceptable in the areas and locations you wish to visit.

Before you travel, also check with the travel agent about dietary customs and cuisine of your honeymoon destination. The phrase "Don't drink the water," in certain circumstances holds a lot of truth. It also applies to water-based edibles such as ice and soups.

Currency and Payment

Travelers' checks will come in handy throughout the honeymoon, but rely more on international credit cards such as American Express, Visa, and Master-Card. With travelers' checks you might have to pay a handling fee with each transaction; with the credit cards you won't. Also with the credit cards you won't need to have money converted to the local currency, nor will you have to figure out exchange rates. The billing company will do all that for you. If you are traveling to a foreign country, exchange enough money to handle cab fare at the airport office change facility. Exchange the rest at a full-service bank. The handling fee will be considerably lower. In a pinch, your hotel will change money for you, but probably at a lower rate.

Packing

Packing will be a major portion of your honeymoon plans. You don't have to pack everything you own, nor should you underpack. Be realistic. Take what you know you will need—and leave room in your luggage to handle purchases you'll make on the trip. Shopping is one of the honeymoon adventures you'll really enjoy.

If you are going to bring small electrical appliances, such as a hair drier or travel iron, call the hotel first. Chances are the room comes with both, so there's no need to pack one. Should you be traveling to a foreign country, be sure to bring electrical adapters.

Other "must-packs" are:

- Cameras and film (Be sure to have them inspected by hand, not by machine, at the airports. The X-ray security device can ruin your film.)
- Extra medication and duplicate prescriptions from your doctor in the event that you need a replacement or refill while away. (The same goes for your eyeglasses prescription.)
- Pocket calculator to handle currency exchanges
- Address book (It comes in handy when writing out postcards.)
- Lists of all credit card and traveler's check numbers; luggage contents; people and phone numbers to call in case of emergencies; passports, visa, driver's license, and other forms of identification; medical coverage and homeowner's insurance identification cards to get you through any possible emergencies

Finally, give a complete copy of your travel schedule to at least two people at home. A family member and close friend will do, just so that there is someone who knows how to get in touch with you should it be necessary. Also be sure to give a final notice to whoever is supposed to pick you up at the airport or cruise pier. Being stranded is not the best way to end your otherwise wonderful honeymoon.

HYPHENATING
CHANGING YOUR NAME

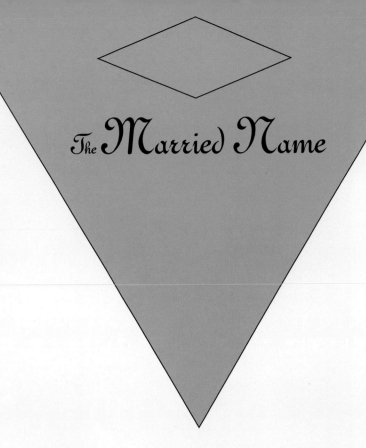

The Married Name

"*What's in a name?*" *Juliet inquires of Romeo in* Shakespeare's classic play. She then asks him to cast off his name. Of course he doesn't, but how times have changed! Whereas Juliet asked Romeo to make that sacrifice to prevent a war, today the matter of a bride changing her name can begin a domestic battle. To paraphrase the Bard, "To change or not to change, that is the question."

Should you change your name? It's up to you, but either way, make sure the matter is discussed. There's no law that says a wife has to take on her husband's last name; it's just a tradition—and not a worldwide one at that. In some countries, especially in Italy and Spain, the woman maintains her single name after marriage. Any daughters from the marriage take on their mother's maiden name while sons take on their father's last name. In Iceland, the daughters take both the mother's first name and the word "daughter," such as Olgadaughter, or Olga's daughter.

The reasons for retaining a surname can be very personal, such as being an only child who wishes to carry on the family name. It could be for aesthetic reasons—

C H A P T E R 1 4

perhaps his last name doesn't sound well with your first name. You might want to maintain your family name strictly for sentimental reasons, or for professional reasons. Of course, if you want to give your personal life the utmost privacy, continue to use your maiden name professionally and use your married name personally. Unless you are a celebrity, that can be a bit complicated or be considered too extreme, but it's up to you.

Ask your husband how he feels. Explain to him that you are not ashamed to take on his name, but you have your personal reasons. Tell him what they are. He should respect them. If his feelings are hurt, ask him how he would feel if the name-change tradition were reversed, and he had to take on your last name. He should see your point.

Not changing your surname is a personal decision between you and your husband, but telling the world of that decision is another matter. Unless you say otherwise, everyone's going to think you followed the custom of taking his name. Before the wedding, tell friends and family that you have decided to keep your surname or whatever you decide to do. This will save embarrassing moments later. Use your thank-you notes to gently tell the world of your decision. The stationery should be imprinted as you prefer: John Smith and Mary Jones-Smith, or if it is your own informal, Mary Jones or Mary Jones-Smith. Everyone should get the message loud and clear. Don't be offended, however, if at times you are addressed as Mrs. Smith. It's done because of tradition, not intolerance.

HYPHENATING

It's become popular in professional circles for a woman to maintain her maiden name but also take on her husband's last name through hyphenation. This can be complicated, particularly when you are connecting two very long names such as Weatherforderner-Bonavitacola or two names that just don't quite sound right together.

For the sake of argument, let's say you decide to

© Bill Horsman

Courtesy of Jerry and Elka Levinrad

Even after the thank-you notes have been mailed, the honeymoon bags unpacked, and life returns to "normal," your wedding is still not "over." It will live forever in your mind and heart, if not in photographs and videotapes. Your wedding is your fairy tale. Live happily ever after.

hyphenate your maiden name with his last name and it looks and sounds wonderful, such as Worthington-Smith. What if you have children? Will they have the last name Smith (his last name) or Worthington-Smith (your last name)? That should be discussed before the issue arises.

Beginning in the mid-eighties, children were often given hyphenated last names, but that soon got too confusing. Families found it difficult to have two last names in one household, schools found it difficult to handle the hyphenated names on official records, including class lists—plus the children themselves found it difficult to handle. Sociologists often wonder what the name situation will become when two children with hyphenated last names marry. Does she then take on yet another hyphen and become Mary Worthington-Smith-Wilson? Or, what if Mary Worthington-Smith marries a man who also has a hyphenated last name? Is she then Mary Worthington-Smith-Wilson-Clarksboro? Put that on an application form!

If you decide to retain your maiden name, that's all well and good, but be more considerate when it comes to children. Sameness is part of childhood saneness. Psychiatrists feel it is best if the child has one last name, and preferably one that is identical to that of one parent—if not both. If you should keep your maiden name and the children take on your husband's last name, don't be surprised if people who don't know you think you are divorced or an unwed mother. That's a price you'll have to pay for your independence.

Changing Your Name

Taking on his name may seem like the ultimate way to show you're together to the end, but it's more complicated than just saying "I do." A change of name changes your whole identity—legally speaking. With that one decision, you're going to have to notify dozens of agencies to get the record(s) right.

Your driver's license will have to be changed, thus you must notify your state's Department of Motor Vehicles in writing. Your social security card will need a change, so another written form is completed at the local Social Security office. Frankly, every piece of identification you carry now has to be changed unless you want to use your maiden name on some items and your married one on others. Some married women take that route when it comes to credit cards. Since it is virtually impossible for a married woman to get a credit card just under her married name—that is, not a joint card with her husband—many women choose not to change their names on credit cards or individual bank accounts. The stores and banks don't care what name you use. As far as they're concerned, you are a number, be it a credit card or a savings or checking account number. As long as that number is in good credit standing, that's all that counts.

Maintaining separate financial accounts can give you better control of your own expenses and spending. It can also be a lifesaver—financially speaking—if you get divorced or if as a couple you run into serious financial problems, such as bankruptcy.

A final word about name changing. Notify your local post office in writing that mail addressed to you under either name should be delivered to your address. If they don't have such a card on file, then mail addressed to your maiden name may not be delivered since the post office's records show no one with that name is registered at your home.

© FPG International

Index